Design and Launch an Online

Social Networking Business

in a WEEK

Other Titles in the Click Start Series

Design and Launch an Online Boutique Business in a Week

Design and Launch an Online E-Commerce Business in a Week

Design and Launch an Online Gift Business in a Week

Design and Launch an Online Travel Business in a Week

Design and Launch an Online Web Design Business in a Week

Entrepreneur MAGAZINE'S
CLICKSTARTS

Design and Launch an Online

Social Networking Business

in a WEEK

- ◆ Complete guide to creating your own online, niche community
- ◆ Capture your share of the Facebook, MySpace, and LinkedIn markets
- ◆ Latest social networking tools and features
- ◆ Technical know-how not required

Entrepreneur Press & Julien Sharp

EP
Entrepreneur.
Press

Jere L. Calmes, Publisher
Cover Design: Desktop Miracles
Production and Composition: Eliot House Productions

This publication is designed to provide accurate and authoritative information in regard to the subject matter covered. It is sold with the understanding that the publisher is not engaged in rendering legal, accounting, or other professional services. If legal advice or other expert assistance is required, the services of a competent professional person should be sought.

Computer icon ©Skocko
Hand icon ©newyear2008

Library of Congress Cataloging-in-Publication Data
Sharp, Julien A.
    Click start: design and launch an online social networking business in a week/by Julien A. Sharp.
        p.   cm.   —(Click start series)
    ISBN-13: 978-1-59918-268-1 (alk. paper)
    ISBN-10: 1-59918-268-8
        1. Business enterprises—Computer network resources. 2. New business enterprises—Management. 3. Small business—Management. I. Entrepreneur Media, Inc. II. Title.
    HF54.56.S53 2009
    006.7′540681—dc22   2009000361

Printed in Canada

13 12 11 10 09   10 9 8 7 6 5 4 3 2 1

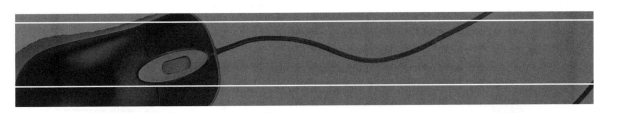

Contents

SECTION I

Building Your Virtual Empire

SECTION IV

Appendices

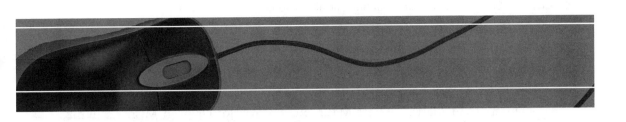

Acknowledgments

I am amazed at how easy it was to contact people while conducting the research for this book. Online networking certainly has made contacting people easier than ever before: a single writer can look up and contact the CEO of a large company (er . . . several CEOs, actually) on the internet, and get a kind response!

Most important, I would like to thank those experts in the field who have been more than generous in sharing their experience and insight:

Stuart Agtsteribbe, Scott Allen, Heather Armstrong, Larry Benet, Gina Bianchini, Peter Bihr, Karen Billipp, Paul Burani, Jere Calmes, Jim Crabbe, Bob Crull, Judy Gitenstein, Heather Graham, Alexander Gutin, Marilyn Jenett, Thad Martin, Elliott Masie, Ross Mayfield, Dr. Ivan Misner, Nikhil Nilakantan, Myra Norton, Jeremiah Owyang, Ted Rheingold, Ron Rubin, Pam Spaulding, Tracy Sullivan, Ray Thompson, Courtney Thurman, Rebekah Tsadik, Kaiser Wahab, Michael Walsh, and Robin Wolaner.

Big kudos also go to my very supportive partner in life, Alix MacLean, who gets a gold star for bringing me all those take-outs—not to mention many iced coffees from Joe's in NYC—while I typed furiously late into the evening.

I would like to say a special thanks to my "office dog" Verdell, who put up with months of very truncated walks and submitted to posing for many pictures as I was building my "tester" online network.

Finally, this book is for my goddaughter Molly Fant and my nieces and nephews Sydney, Jacob, and Grant Beechboard and Sofia Cerasoli, who have never known a time without a home computer, and for whom online networking will be as natural as breathing.

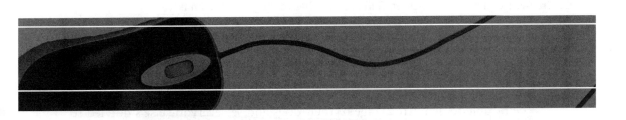

Foreword
by Ted Rheingold, Founder of Dogster.com and Catster.com

*I*n June 2003 I got this funny idea: I thought, since people like sharing and showing off photos of their dogs, why not make a web service so they could show off their dogs online? I realized that although the internet offered most things, there was still no site dedicated to people's dogs. I lied to myself and thought I could crank out a site in a couple of days and would start making money off it soon after that. It took more than a couple days, but it was still the fastest company I've ever built.

Within three months of launching Dogster.com, 30,000 people had made web pages for their dogs, and I was bringing on my first advertisers. I wasn't able to quit my day job for another year, but the pleasure people received from being able to dedicate a page to their dogs and see everyone else's dog led to TV interviews, nationwide newspaper articles, invitations to speak at conferences, and more customers than one person could possibly interact with.

Fast-forward five years and it confounds me how much easier it would be to start such a site today. The digital landscape is awash with amazing and sophisticated tools for building an online networking business. Many require no technical knowledge and have easy hooks for making revenue. And if you're ready to get your hands dirty, you can build almost anything in fewer lines of code than has ever been possible. There are even free or cheap services to help with customer service, software and widgets, video and photo storage . . . you name it.

But be forewarned: The one thing you'll likely never be able to outsource and that will determine the success of your endeavor more than anything is developing, nurturing, and growing your user base from day one. Without happy, involved, engaged customers your beautiful, technically complete social networking service will be an empty city.

Thus, in the end, your goal has to be building a thriving, vibrant community, and a community platform is simply the exoskeleton you'll need so you can really start your business.

When I started Dogster.com, I did not set out to build a social service. I did not expect that people would want social networking functionality (not that that was even a term at the time). But what made the difference, I believe, is that I listened to the early site visitors as closely as possible. Within a month, I knew I had to throw out the road map I had envisioned before the site was launched and should focus all my energies on doing everything I could to meet the needs of the customers that were already here.

One of the biggest benefits of offering a customer-focused product on the web is that you'll have no shortage of opportunities to hear from them. Consider it free market research; and free QA, copyediting, and product planning. Even the biggest insult or complaint can be reversed to become a statement about how you can improve things to make your customers happier.

And when you have happy customers, they tell everyone they know and then, suddenly, you have an army of free marketers and PR people telling your story for you.

So while social networking tools, services, and software have become commodities, something to be bought, sold, or traded, the thriving, growing community of customers is the rare thing that will be the true determinant of your business's value. Thus, while it's easy early on to believe the most important place to focus your attention is on building the right set of features, where your attention should always be is on getting your site in front of prospective customers.

Your chief concerns should be: How can I find out what they like and don't like? How can I get my first 10,000 registrants, so I can know if I can get it to 100,000, 1,000,000, or more? The business of your business then will be bringing those people together and making sure they have an ideal time every time they visit the site.

However, while it is very important to make the interaction between visitor and web service as pleasing as possible, the most important thing is to make interaction and networking among the visitors themselves as efficient and pleasurable as possible—that is your business.

I once got some very good advice, which I literally used to decide whether to start Dogster in the first place. The advice was: "Right now is the right time to be starting on the next big thing." This evergreen truism will never be false. So you haven't missed the boat, nor has the opportunity passed you by. When you think you have the perfect plan, go for it.

—Ted Rheingold
Founder, Dogster.com and Catster.com
June 2008

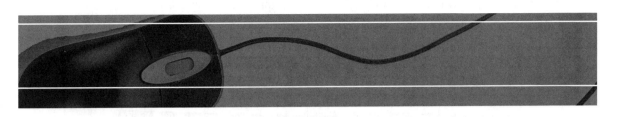

Preface

*T*here has never been a better time to be an internet entrepreneur! Thanks to Moore's Law, technology is progressing at lightning speeds, costs of online storage and bandwidth are decreasing at the same rate, and we now have a generation of consumers who have never known a time without computers and the internet.

MOORE'S LAW

This concept was developed and explained by Intel co-founder Gordon Moore in a paper he wrote in 1965. He stated that the number of transistors on a chip, or the amount of data, etc. a computer chip can hold, will double about every two years. At the same time, the price for such chips will decrease. This concept is easily understood when considering the newest mp3 players and microcomputers, and even the newest smart phones with their staggering capabilities.

The exciting part is that rather than saturating the market, every new technological breakthrough opens the door for additional types of internet-based businesses. The savvy entrepreneur can be set up for life by keeping up with, and taking advantage of, the latest opportunities. Right now, one of the best opportunities is online networking.

Why This Book Is for You

You may be a victim of downsizing or outsourcing and want to be in control of your own destiny from now on. When it's your business, you can't get laid off or fired! Or your spouse or partner relocated and you need to find new employment . . . now might be a perfect time to start a business instead of a job search. You may have already started one, or more, internet-based businesses over the years and want to profit from the incredible new revenue-generating opportunities that have sprung up for developers and creators of online networks. Or it just might be that you have spent a lot of time in online communities and have some great ideas for a better one!

The thing is, there are so many options for tapping into this business that there is something for everyone! You can start your online network and still keep your day job as you begin to grow it. Or you can jump into it full time. It's completely up to you.

Successful entrepreneurs must be by nature good at networking, and many business networkers have flocked into the world of virtual networking. For the younger generations, online networking (whether for business or just to keep in touch with friends) is a native skill. If you are between the ages of 28 and 45, you have spent much, if not all, of your working life using the internet in some form. Those of you nearing the older end of the range have been able to observe the internet from its inception. You will have seen the money-making opportunities that have come from the internet's ever-expanding capabilities.

Many of you will almost certainly be a member of one and likely several online networking communities. You may already have made a profile on LinkedIn or other similar online business networking sites. You may have a profile on Facebook or MySpace (today considered to be the most widely used online networking sites in North America). If you have teenagers, they are most certainly on one or both of these two sites. In short, you have some idea what "online networking" is all about, so why not start your own network and make revenue from it?

That's where this book comes in. It can show just about anyone how to get a networking site up and running in a single week; it details everything you will need to get an online networking business designed and ready to go.

In writing this book, we interviewed several successful players in this still very young game who will help solidify the concepts of what it takes to launch your business.

We'll help you understand the basics of online networking and go over all the features available to make your network dynamic and interesting. Then we'll help you develop your own niche in the marketplace and show you how to target your chosen membership. We'll provide you with some of the business basics that you will need to know before you get started, including technological considerations, business setup, and some of the legal aspects of online networking. Finally, we'll teach you how to generate traffic and membership, how to build advertising and other passive revenue streams, and about the (many) platforms available for powering up your online empire.

One major development has eliminated the need to layout huge amounts of cash on technology—the new online software-as-a-service and hosting capabilities now available that make it possible for virtually anyone to set up and run an online social or business networking community. We have highlighted several of these companies in the book.

If you are interested in starting and running a business, particularly an online business, but do not have a clear idea of how to start or much time to set it up, then this book is for you. It will provide a concise step-by-step guide leading right up to your successful launch.

Don't have a lot of capital socked away for investment in your business? You don't need it! Lacking in, shall we say, technical expertise? You don't need that either! At this point in the evolution of the internet it is very possible for almost anyone to design and launch a networking site, easily and affordably; you just need to know the right type of vendors to choose.

Now, you might feel that there are barriers to success in this type of venture. The technological aspects of building a successful online community may intimidate you. Or you might not fully believe that such a business could be designed and launched in a week. You may not feel you could compete with the bigger, more established companies for a profitable share of available members and revenue. But the major hurdle of development is no longer a concern. There is a multitude of online networking businesses to start, but while there is a seemingly ubiquitous number of the well-established sites, the market is far from saturated.

The Easiest—and Quickest—Business You'll Ever Start

Many people became successful during the first wave of internet businesses. But a whole new wave of opportunity has just begun to flow, and with the emergence of the new technology there are incredible opportunities to reach the heights of professional and financial success.

With the right tools, knowledge, self-discipline, and perseverance, starting an online networking business is one of the best ways to achieve financial success through the internet and to become the master of your own professional universe.

Are you ready to see what it's all about? Read on . . . we look forward to seeing your network soon among the industry's top online networking sites!

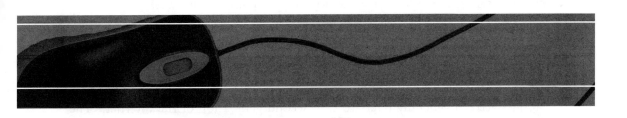

Introduction

*I*n the span of just a few years, we evolved from a world in which people had never heard of the internet to one in which virtually every business has a website and e-mail has become the desired form of personal and business communication. As things evolved, the technology became easier to use, and individuals developed their own websites to post information about themselves, families, jobs, hobbies, pets, etc. For the most part, however, these websites were generally stagnant, with fixed content and infrequent changes. Then along came Web 2.0, and a whole lot of changes were in store!

Web 2.0 generally refers to the "second generation of the internet." The internet has improved over time, and has developed ever more elaborate capabilities. This has had a huge impact on both business and individual internet users.

In a Web 2.0 world, there is much more emphasis on user-generated content (UCG). By this, we mean content (including, but not limited to, commentary, news reports, videos, photos, and captions) that is produced by the general public, as opposed to being compiled, written, and published by traditional media professionals.

There are also so many more services available that allow people to collaborate and share information online. For example, Web 2.0 has allowed simple message boards to become full-blown online diaries—also known as blogs (or weblogs)—which could be regularly updated.

People now spend a lot more time sitting at computers, whether for work or play. The need for "community" in a virtual society is strongly felt by many—the isolated behavior of sitting at a computer focused on the screen has forced the development of communities through use of the very machine that initially eliminated them! This sense of a lack of community resulted in a literal "blog explosion": people creating and maintaining their own blogs now number in the millions worldwide.

One of the common features of blogs is the "comments" section, where readers can post comments about their thoughts on a particular post. Following comment threads, you can get a general sense of which participants were more "connected" with each other. People become connected by virtue of a common

> ## Words of Wisdom
>
> *A community can form even from people making comments to a blog post. I have allowed comments on the Daily Photo section of my blog, and people who commented there became friends, kept in touch outside of the scope of my blog, and have even seen each other in person. I absolutely think community is the way to go.*
>
> —HEATHER ARMSTRONG, AUTHOR OF THE AWARD-WINNING BLOG DOOCE (DOOCE.COM), A SITE WITH WELL OVER 1,000,000 PAGE VIEWS PER MONTH

interest that they publicly write about in the blog. Such interaction has enabled many online communities to develop . . . simply from the comment threads. And the blog was a natural precursor to the explosion of online networks.

The communities that sprung up on blogs, web forums, and message boards have now evolved into social networking sites. Some of the best known are LinkedIn (linkedin.com), MySpace (myspace.com), and Facebook (facebook.com) and they have proven that networking sites can generate substantial revenue in a revolutionary business model.

According to comScore Inc. (comscore.com), in 2008—about 120.3 million internet users (making up approximately two-thirds of the total internet audience) visited social networking websites. A report released by the Pew Internet & American Life Project in January 2009 found that the percentage of adult internet users (aged 18 and over) who have at least one profile on a social networking site *has more than quadrupled* over the past four years. Between 2005 to the end of 2008, that use went from 8 to 35 percent!

As of May 2008, LinkedIn logged over 20 million registered users, spanning 150 industries. As the economy went into a tailspin throughout 2008, more and more users signed on to sites such as LinkedIn. According to an October 2008 article by Tony Ha for *Venture Beat* ("Shaky Economy Drives Users to LinkedIn"), the online networking site reported the following:

➡ 50 percent increase in site usage by financial industry members
➡ 14 percent increase in recommendations
➡ 10 percent increase in invitations sent
➡ 7 percent increase in sign-ups
➡ 9 percent increase in page views
➡ 11 percent increase in the number of connections being made

Scott Allen and David Teten, co-authors of *The Virtual Handshake*, have also identified the trend:

The potential market for business networking is enormous. Over 20 million businesses worldwide are members of local chambers of commerce. Add to that all the marketing, business development, and non-retail sales professionals, plus hiring managers, recruiters, and job seekers, and the number gets very large.

Generating revenue and supporting other business processes via relationships are as compelling reasons to connect as finding old schoolmates or potential dating partners.

Nearly half of all U.S. internet users have created some form of—as Teten and Allen call it—"virtual presence" simply by posting a picture or story to a website, creating a blog, or joining an online forum.

This need for self-expression on the internet has transformed the way people use it to follow their entrepreneurial dreams. The internet business model has become ever more complex as there are now many avenues through which a single entrepreneur can run her own business, pay herself a salary, and bring a certain flexibility to her life. And there is room in the market for a seemingly infinite number of internet businesses. Chris Anderson, editor-in-chief of *Wired* magazine and former U.S. business editor of *The Economist*, coined the expression "the long tail." (No term could be more apt as far as helping us understand the growth of smaller businesses on the internet, many of which would never have survived—or perhaps ever been started at all—in the formerly mass-market-dominated business models.) He first introduced the term in a

NO-COST PUBLISHING: A 21ST CENTURY REALITY

Ross Mayfield, Chairman, CEO, and co-founder of Socialtext, a company that writes "social software" packages for businesses, is a respected expert in the field of online networking. At a recent forum, he discussed some of the major changes that have contributed to the wave of online networks:

1. Identity expression is now more common on the web. (This is true especially with teens, but we are all gradually becoming more comfortable with the concept of "transparency.")

2. The cost of global publishing has fallen to zero.

3. The cost of group forming has fallen to zero, and this is perhaps even more important than publishing.

2004 article in *Wired* magazine. In turn, that article became one of the most cited in the history of the magazine. In very brief summary, the long tail refers to a business strategy: selling a large number of unique items (or services) in "relatively small quantities."

Amazon.com and Netflix are great examples of proponents of the long tail strategy, and are commonly used in the explanation of the term. A book store can stock only a finite number of books on its shelves, so must choose only those that are most likely to sell. As an online store, Amazon.com can cater to the most unique whims of its clients because the "store" is virtual. In his book, also titled *The Long Tail*, Anderson states that "the mass market is turning into a mass of niches."

But what does this mean to you as an entrepreneur considering starting an online networking business? It means that you, a single person sitting at a computer, can start an online network in an area that, without the concept of niche marketing, would be completely dominated by the relatively small number of "big guys" such as Facebook, MySpace, LinkedIn, and a few others. These networks are certainly extremely popular and attract millions of members, but *the majority of online (social) networks are much smaller, focusing on single "niche" interests!* All you have to do is find your niche. Armed with this book, you'll be able to consider what type of audience you want to attract, and get easily set up in no time.

With the number of software packages and network-building platforms now available on the market, anyone with a computer and a high-speed internet connection can design and launch an online networking business in under a week. In fact, many of the available software platforms can have you up and running in under an hour!

Because any business dealing with the internet is changing at lightning speed, information changes daily. This book was researched and written over a period of about six and a half months, and during that time, countless new products and services—not to mention new networks—were introduced—literally every day. To put into something so finite as a book all the available options for this business isn't only impossible, it is impractical.

Thus, we have endeavored to write this book as a launching pad for entrepreneurs interested in tapping into a revenue stream that gets others (the members of the network) to do the work.

As you create your network, you will learn how easy it is to find information on the internet. We have included several websites (blogs, networks, and general information sites) and web addresses in the Resources section and throughout the book. As you go forward with your business, *do not be afraid to ask others who have done this already*! The virtual world is an open-source one, and thanks to the vision of people like Tim Burners-Lee, credited with creating the web and who always meant for it to be a "social" experience, it is a world where everyone can contribute to the growth of others for the benefit of all.

Building Your Virtual Empire

Chapter 1

Online Networks and What People Do on Them

*T*he term "social networking" may be somewhat confusing to an entrepreneur wanting to build an online networking business. After all, "social" is fun, right? And social networks are for kids making "friends" on Facebook or Myspace, aren't they? Not necessarily—and certainly not exclusively.

Wikipedia defines social networks as "communities of people who share interests and activities or who are interested in exploring the interests and activities of others." Another popular

Words of Wisdom

When Tim Burners-Lee created the web what he had in mind wasn't the browser. He thought we would be using it with our own editing capabilities, and everyone would be contributing content and media. That's kind of close to where we are today.

—Ross Mayfield, Chairman, President,
and Co-Founder, Socialtext

definition is "a map of the relationships between individuals." Add a computer, internet connection, and some user-friendly software to that, and you have an online network: a place to build relationships in the virtual (or online) world.

But how does this relate to you? And how can it relate to your bottom line if you want to start a business in this still very new area?

Online networks allow users (or members) to interact and connect in cyberspace in entirely new ways, using various user-friendly features including blogging, spoken or written live "chat" sessions, instant messaging (IM), mail, video, or photo sharing, and commenting on or even editing content that has been uploaded by other people. Such means of connectivity have forever changed the way in which we share information.

They have also made the world a much smaller place. Students who, several years ago, might have become "pen pals" with their peers in other countries can now "meet" them via video chat or view their online profiles posted on networks. A businessperson can quickly view the LinkedIn profile of a prospective vendor (or perhaps even a prospective employee), see recommendations written about them, view their resume or other profile information, and, in many cases, even see what he or she looks like.

Ted Rheingold, founder of Dogster (dogster.com) and Catster (catster .com), started his online (social) networking site in 2004 as a place where users could upload pictures of their dogs onto their own "pages" instead of sending e-mails with attached photos. In a few short years, these two sites have grown into enormously popular "meeting" places for pet owners. Members communicate with each other in the online forum, and now share not just photos but also videos, stories, and advice.

The sites earn money from advertising revenues and "premium" membership packages (as with many networks, a basic membership is free). Rheingold describes the sites as a "microcosm of what is happening on the internet"—like-minded people have found a place to meet and connect with other people with the same interest.

(We'll talk more about Dogster.com later in the book. It's a great example of what you can do with a little creativity and the willingness to listen to your customers as you grow!)

The themes around which you could build a social network are virtually unlimited. But to get you going, here are a few of the literally infinite possibilities:

➡ You could create a network around a favorite celebrity and build a network of fans.

➡ You may be a performing artist, and want to grow your brand and sell your songs through your network. Thousands of independent artists are promoting themselves through online networking sites, with far greater success than they may have had in getting that elusive "record deal" from a major label.

➡ You could set up a not-for-profit business built completely around a network where you can encourage others to get involved in your cause, donate, and even purchase items from an online store.

➡ Just as "mommy blogging" (see sidebar) has raked in the ad dollars over the past few years, parenting networks with tips, interaction between members, and, of course, cute baby photos and stories uploaded by the members have launched the network creators into the

MOMS RULE IN THE BLOGOSHERE!

One of the fastest-growing (if not the fastest) demographics on social networks is . . . moms. That's right: Mothers in the age range of 35 to 45 are posting pictures and making family "home pages" to share with relatives and friends. They are "pimping" (Myspace-generation speak for "decorating") their pages, making slide shows of their photos . . . they are even using "widgets" (applications, or mini-programs, that you can embed into a website or a blog).

stratosphere, drawing high-profile—not to mention high-paying—advertisers to their sites!

➡ Suppose you are running an event or conference. Adding an online networking component to your plans could allow attendees to meet each other before the event, and to share photos and contact information after. You could charge people an access fee for this as a "premium" over and above the conference fees, gaining additional revenues.

➡ By creating an online network you can turn your favorite hobby into a business. If you form an inviting, easy-to-navigate place for others who share your interest in, say, cars, biking, travel, sports, fashion, books, movies, DIY, crafts, cooking, fishing . . . you could grow a community to a size that would attract the attention of advertisers wanting to get their products in front of a targeted group of potential customers.

➡ Do you have a business already? Whether you have a large corporation or a small business, adding an online networking component can be a big boost to your bottom line. You can highlight new products or services, generate buzz about your brand, and answer your customers' questions or concerns.

Other types of networks gaining traction include: career- and job-search advice; pet networks; classmate connectors or reunion networks; homeowner or neighborhood sites; networks that facilitate "how-to" or other educational interaction; support group networks for health or other major life issues. All you have to do is discover what resonates with you and your goals, and you can get a site up and running within a week.

We can already hear you asking, "Can I really do this in a week?" Actually, the title of this book is a bit of a misnomer. You don't need a week to design and launch an online networking business: you can do that part in an *hour*. Creating a basic networking site can be done in less time than it takes to heat a frozen pizza in the oven. Other entrepreneurs have developed the resources to make it easy for you!

Way Beyond Color Schemes

If you ever visit Blogger (blogger.com), a widely popular platform owned by Google that allows you to create your own blogs in minutes, and do a random

search of the blogs using that platform, you will see many that have been created and left to sit, unchanged and unvisited for weeks, months, even years.

At the time of this writing, Technorati (technorati.com), an internet
search engine for searching blogs, is tracking 112.8 million blogs and more
than 250 million pieces of tagged social media (also commonly referred to as
"citizen media"). Yes, you read it correctly—*millions*. When blogs started to
take off, it became easy for virtually anyone to launch one, and as many of the
popular blogging platforms (including Blogger) are completely free, launching required no financial outlay.

Today, it is just as easy to create your own online network. But you don't
want a site with no users or members, that ends up in the cyber-graveyard as
so many websites have done. So while it is possible to design your network in
an hour or less, you will want to spend the rest of your week making sure that
you do the proper planning:

1. Is this going to be a part-time or full-time venture?
2. Are you going to have money to invest or will you start with a smaller
   budget?
3. What technology (hardware and software) will you need? Do you
   already have it, or must you acquire it before launching?
4. What type of access will you provide? Will your community be "gated"
   or completely open to anyone?
5. What is your plan for earning money? Will you provide a completely
   free site and support yourself by selling advertising? Will you offer
   "premium" services for a fee? Will you attach an online store, or maybe
   join affiliate programs with other stores?
6. What software- or network-hosting platform will you use?
7. Is your community only for "virtual" networking or will you encourage
   or formulate an "in person" component?
8. What is your network's *purpose*? What type of people do you want to
   join your community?

Point number 8 is perhaps the most important thing to consider: *People
join a network to grow their contacts and build relationships.* They want to have
another source for leads or referrals and meet prospective clients or business
associates. They want to build their business. They want to make friends with

people who share a common interest. Maybe they want to find a date. Even though the medium for this networking is online, it still takes time and effort to make it work, just as "face-to-face" networking does. So the people who come to your business will need to believe that the community is a fit for them and will help them with their own networking goals—and they need to believe this quickly.

Today's networks can offer so many features that are not only fun to use, but also keep people engaged in your network, which means higher traffic and greater ad revenues.

If you take some time to plan your network carefully, people will visit it over and over, and even more important, they will bring their friends or business associates, who will in turn bring their acquaintances . . . and so on!

Chapter 2

Features of an Online Network

*T*he community you create will likely have all, or certainly most, of the following features: Forums (discussion rooms), blogs (online web diaries), chat features, and video and photo capabilities. If you are more technically savvy (or have the resources to hire a technical-support staff member or team) you might even be able to offer wiki (user-edited content area) capability.

Even if you've browsed your way around a network or two as a member, the sheer number of features available can be a little bit overwhelming. So to help you out, we've researched and compiled a list of features commonly used by administrators and members of online networks. Most of these come standard in today's software-as-a-service and stand-alone packages, but if some are particularly important to your plans, make sure the package you are considering offers them.

(Note: Keep in mind that some companies sell extra features in modules at an extra fee, while others offer them for free.)

➡ *Administrative control.* Allows network owner to monitor and manage all content uploaded by members, and gives the ability to delete material deemed offensive or otherwise out of sync with the overall theme of the network.

➡ *Advertising.* Provides network owners the ability to run their own ads on the network, including installing Google AdSense.

➡ *Aggregation pages.* Members can browse content across the network.

➡ *Badges.* Networks can design and embed graphics on other sites, used to promote the network across the internet.

➡ *Blogging.* Members can create and update their own online diaries, including content, embedded photos, and videos (in most cases). For the most part, blogs are driven by the comments readers make about the different entries (or "blog posts"). Figure 2.1 shows some examples of blogs available on Dogster.com.

➡ *Broadcasts.* Allows members (or the administrator) to send a single message to their choice of multiple users.

➡ *Chat* (also known as instant messaging, or IM). Allows members to communicate in real time and to set up their own chat rooms to interact in a real-time environment.

➡ *Comments.* Allows members to post comments to blog posts, photos, videos, or other members.

➡ *Content management.* Allows the administrator to keep the network secure and safe—includes spam (or profanity) filters, COPPA-compliant features, and user moderation.

➡ *Customization.* Allows members to individualize their pages (or the groups they create) with different templates, backgrounds, colors, and

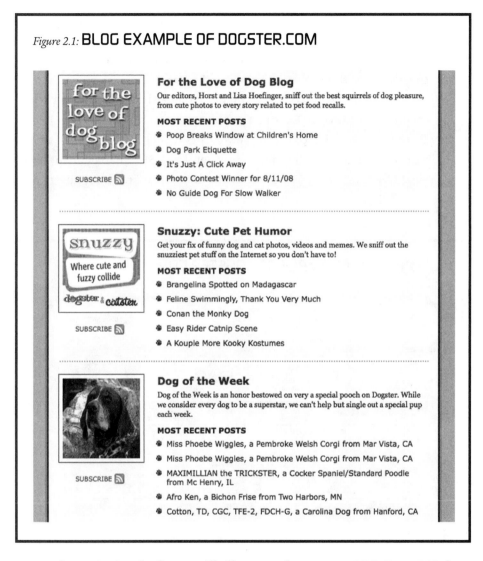

Figure 2.1: BLOG EXAMPLE OF DOGSTER.COM

For the Love of Dog Blog

Our editors, Horst and Lisa Hoefinger, sniff out the best squirrels of dog pleasure, from cute photos to every story related to pet food recalls.

MOST RECENT POSTS

* Poop Breaks Window at Children's Home
* Dog Park Etiquette
* It's Just A Click Away
* Photo Contest Winner for 8/11/08
* No Guide Dog For Slow Walker

SUBSCRIBE

Snuzzy: Cute Pet Humor

Get your fix of funny dog and cat photos, videos and memes. We sniff out the snuzziest pet stuff on the Internet so you don't have to!

MOST RECENT POSTS

* Brangelina Spotted on Madagascar
* Feline Swimmingly, Thank You Very Much
* Conan the Monky Dog
* Easy Rider Catnip Scene
* A Kouple More Kooky Kostumes

SUBSCRIBE

Dog of the Week

Dog of the Week is an honor bestowed on very a special pooch on Dogster. While we consider every dog to be a superstar, we can't help but single out a special pup each week.

MOST RECENT POSTS

* Miss Phoebe Wiggles, a Pembroke Welsh Corgi from Mar Vista, CA
* Miss Phoebe Wiggles, a Pembroke Welsh Corgi from Mar Vista, CA
* MAXIMILLIAN the TRICKSTER, a Cocker Spaniel/Standard Poodle from Mc Henry, IL
* Afro Ken, a Bichon Frise from Two Harbors, MN
* Cotton, TD, CGC, TFE-2, FDCH-G, a Carolina Dog from Hanford, CA

SUBSCRIBE

fonts. Some platforms will allow members to use HTML or CSS for a fully customized look.

➡ *Discussion boards (forums).* Online, virtual "bulletin boards" formed around a variety of activities or interests. The discussion is also called a "thread"; it is started by one user and other users then respond. It allows members to initiate a discussion on a topic of their choice.

Discussion boards should allow the administrator to have final control over the content in the forums (see Moderation). Dogster.com has many different forums for its members, most of which were started by the members themselves as shown in Figure 2.2.

➡ *Embeddable media.* Links video and photo slide show broadcasts back to the network (as opposed to an outside video or photo service).

➡ *Events.* Allows users to create new events, which can be public or private; other features include: event calendar, RSVP management, easy-view of events hosted or attended by members, and integration with Google Maps.

Figure 2.2: **FORUM EXAMPLE OF DOGSTER.COM**

Forums Home > **Main Topics**   `quick search` 🔍

Informative Topics	Threads	Posts	Hot & New Topics
Dog Health	12779	126261	Hot! How much do you pay for heartworm test? (33) New! Every 3 weeks is killing me! (Today 1:19 pm)
Food & Nutrition	7394	91902	Hot! What do you think of this food? (49) New! EVO and water intake (Today 1:27 pm)
Raw Food Diet	2483	34144	Hot! Green tripe! GREEN TRIPE!!! (19) New! Payoff (Today 12:57 pm)
Home Prepared Food & Recipes	610	5215	Hot! Help (5) New! anyone use fish in their home cooked recipes? (Today 6:47 am)
Behavior & Training	10296	107113	Hot! Bark it up! What do you do that is "bad" Pawrenting (49) New! Why small dogs need to be socialized (Today 1:32 pm)
Puppy Place	1934	20732	Hot! thoughts? (18) New! My baby is waiting! (Today 1:26 pm)
Choosing the Right Dog	1598	28134	Hot! What's my other breed? (15) New! Looking to show? (Today 1:29 pm)
Adoption & Happy Endings	2098	12976	Hot! These dogs desperately need your help (scheduled to die Friday) (7) New! These dogs desperately need your help (scheduled to die Friday) (Today 1:08 pm)

➡ *Forums.* See Discussion boards.

➡ *Groups.* Allows members to join specific groups within an online network, based on a shared interest or topic. Figure 2.3 shows a few of the (many) groups open to members of LearningTown.com (this is explored further in Chapter 5).

➡ *Instant messaging (IM).* See Chat.

➡ *Integration.* Allows members to share content between the network and their profile pages on several other "mainstream" networks.

➡ *Mail.* Allows composing, sending, reading, deleting private or group messages to and from members and administrators or moderators.

➡ *Media capacities.* Includes, but is not limited to, a streaming audio and video player, photo gallery, blogs and vlogs (video blogs). With shared media capacities, members in a group can post items to shared media outlets.

➡ *Member services.* The following capabilities are a given for online networking communities:

· Accept/decline invitations
· Preview member profiles
· Invite others to join
· Create new groups
· Post bulletins
· Easily invite other members to connect

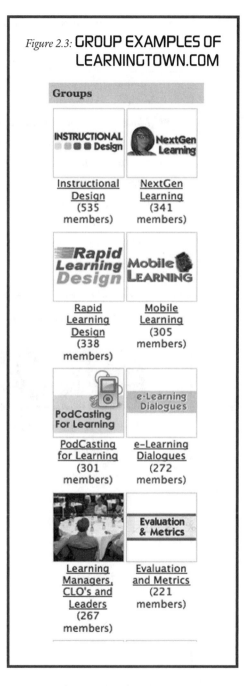

Figure 2.3: **GROUP EXAMPLES OF LEARNINGTOWN.COM**

· Fast and easy registration for members

➡ *Message board.* Allows group owners (as well as network owners and moderators) to create multiple messages for members of that group.

➡ *Mobile uploads.* Allows members to upload photos, blog posts, and other content directly to the network.

➡ *Moderation (users or content).* Allows network owners or administrators to issue warnings or suspensions to members who violate the rules of the network, and provides the ability to permanently ban violators and delete offensive content. The online networking software platform Ning (ning.com) has extensive privacy and control features to allow its administrators/owners close moderation over their networks. Examples of these are shown in Figure 2.4, at UrbanDog.com.

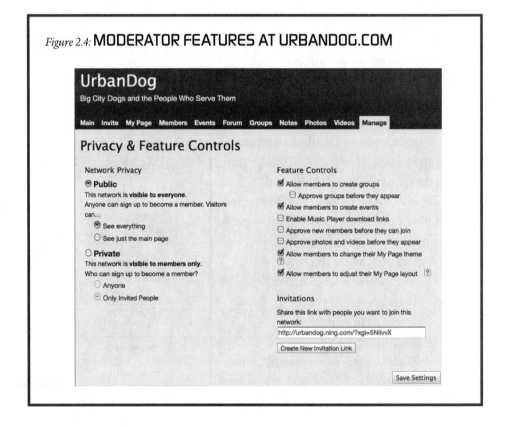

Figure 2.4: **MODERATOR FEATURES AT URBANDOG.COM**

- *Moderators.* Gives network owners the ability to assign moderators or subadministrators to help monitor the network's content (see Moderation).
- *Network.* Foundation of social or online networks: allows users/members to build a group of other members (think of "connections" in LinkedIn or "friends" on Facebook or MySpace).
- *Permissions.* Allows network owners to change privacy settings at any time. Subgroups, networks, or profile pages can also be set to "public" (open to public view) or "private" (viewable by invitation for specific members only).
- *Photo gallery.* Allows members to create their own photo galleries (for example, flickr.com) and upload photos to the page via internet or other connection (see Mobile uploads). Other capabilities can include: creating tags (keywords) for photos, rating and/or featuring certain photos, and allowing members to submit comments to photos.
- *Podcasts.* A user-generated media file (audio or video) distributed over the internet using syndication feeds, for playback on portable media players and personal computers.
- *Privacy and security.* Allows members to set certain pages (or their entire profiles) to be viewable to anyone on the network, their connections only, or just themselves.
- *Profile.* Allows new members to create their own personal profile and decide who can "view" their profile—all of the network, or only "friends" or other allowed members. A good platform will allow members' basic profiles to be easily extended and adapted and network owners to completely customize the profile fields in the profile at their discretion, based on the purpose of the network.
- *Search engine optimized (SEO) URLs.* A platform or software that will submit the URLs (web address) of networks using its service to major search engines—a very important service for those wanting to generate an income from the network or just wanting to make sure potential members can find the network in a search.
- *Search functionality.* Allows members to generate specific content or member searches (many platforms have a "who's online" feature).

➡ *Setup assistant.* Streamlines the process of setting up an entire online network.

➡ *Statistics tracking.* Allows owners to track for revenue and planning purposes. Important items to track include: traffic to the site; number of members signing up; most heavily viewed content on the network (see Chapter 9).

➡ *Surveys.* Allows owners to obtain accurate member feedback; many software packages and platforms have this feature built in to the administrative package.

➡ *System messages.* Allows network owners or administrators to compile and automatically or manually send messages to all members, or to specific members (such as new sign-ups).

➡ *Tagging and rating.* Provides the capability for members to tag and rate content, making ranking content across the network very easy.

➡ *Trial period/demo.* Allows network owners to trial a package before completing the purchase. Some companies offer free network setup (usually with premium options at a fee), while others charge for the software and additional components.

➡ *Video uploads (video sharing).* Allows members to upload videos to the network (as in YouTube.com); some software packages or platforms accept videos in virtually any format while others have more limited capabilities.

➡ *Widgets.* Mini-applications that can be embedded into a website or a blog, such as blogroll or scrolling headlines; offers "free advertising" for the originator.

➡ *Wikis.* Web pages that are editable by any reader, using simple linking and formatting commands rather than requiring people to learn HTML.

Chapter 3

Defining Your Community

*T*here are three elements you need to consider when setting up your online network: technology, design, and community. Elliott Masie is the CEO of the Masie Center & Learning Consortium, a think tank that examines the topics of technology, learning, business, and productivity in the workplace. According to Masie, it is important to separate a network's technology dimensions from the design and community dimensions. And it is vital that you consider the elements of design and community first.

The following are some points to consider before launching your network:

- What is the *focus* of your network? Are you using it to facilitate meetings in the "real world"? Are you using it to promote a product or service you already offer? Are you making a network to gather people in a certain interest, lifestyle, or political niche?
- What is your *target user group*? What is the age range of members you are hoping to attract? Will the site target women or men, stay-at-home or working moms specifically? Is your site aimed at businesspeople or at those seeking to socialize online—or a combination of both?
- Will you operate as a one-person show or will you hire people to help with the administration of your site or management of your community?
- What features will you offer, particularly in the first few weeks and months of your network?
- Have you provided a *reason* for people to join your network?
- Do you have existing contacts (friends or business associates) that will help you get your network off the ground?
- How will you continue to attract new people to your network?

CLICK TIP

Poor design is one of the most common causes of network failure. Many people think they just have to "build" a site, rather than design it. But ask yourself these questions: Why would someone want to come to your site? What are you hosting? Is your site going to merely be what Masie calls a "town square"—a place where people can find each other? Or do you want to offer your members discussions, forums, or even opportunities for self-publishing (videos, blogs, vlogs)? The answers to these questions will determine the level of design needed for your site.

You might want to make your network a sort of "portal" to other content. It could be a virtual magazine, with front- and back-page content and filler, supplied by you, your writing team, or even the members of your network themselves. You might head in a different direction entirely, starting a little smaller and building what is basically a website with a "networking" component.

To achieve your specific ends, the design of our site is crucial. It is not dissimilar to interior design, decorating, or even planning a meal: You have to find the right mix to satisfy your members and your advertisers.

And who *are* your members going to be? This is where the concept of *community* comes in.

➡ *Are your members going to be mostly young?* Then you'll definitely want a link to Facebook and MySpace—most of your potential members will already have a profile on both of those sites. You will also want to have the most up-to-date media features, as the young are typically already experts at sharing photos and videos.

DON'T DISREGARD THE BABY BOOMERS

A report by the Pew Internet & American Life Project (January 2009) provides a breakdown of social/online networking users by age. Young adults are still the most likely to use the sites—but boomers are definitely using them. Don't forget this "untapped market" when you plan your community and the users you want to attract!

Percentage of Adults with a Social Networking Profile by Age

Ages 24 to 34	57 percent
Ages 24 to 44	30 percent
Ages 45 to 54	19 percent
Ages 55 to 64	10 percent

➡ *If you are catering to a Gen X audience* with a professional theme, make sure a link to LinkedIn is a prominent feature on the site. The language, too, will need to be less focused on the latest rock group, and more on dialogue for (and by) professionals.

➡ *If you are targeting baby boomers*, bear in mind that many may not fully understand what an online network is. Your site will need to include a lot of training at each step, so you don't lose potential members. They may love what you have to offer, but become intimidated in the process of simply signing up.

> ## Words of Wisdom
>
> *Communities are powerful tools, as long as you put members' needs first.*
>
> —Jeremiah Owyang, Senior Analyst, Forrester Research

If you have never created a website of your own before—much less an entire online network—the choice of software or platform is very important. There are many choices that can, in varying degrees, handle virtually all of the "tech" stuff—leaving you to focus on what will, in the end, be much more important to the long-term success of your business: planning for and continuously addressing the needs of your community.

You're Now a Member of the Media!

When you take your foray into an online networking business, you are actually becoming part of the media industry. The original media companies focused on printed publications: magazines, books, newspapers, etc. In the 20th century we saw the advent of radio, television, and cinema. Now, as we approach the end of the first decade of the new millennium, we have the still-evolving world of internet media.

Robin Wolaner, founder of TeeBeeDee (tbd.com), a social networking site targeted at members aged 40 and above, has spent her entire career in various sectors of the media. Prior to starting her fast-growing network, she was the founder of *Parenting* magazine, held senior positions in both print and online media corporations, and is an accomplished author and speaker. During a speech she gave at a forum in April 2008, she said, "If a lot of people are 'on' [registered, members of] a site but not really 'using' it, it cannot be a true media company. Good media companies come from understanding a market need."

To succeed with your media company—your online network—you must be *genuine*. To make a site genuine, it must demonstrate a very clear understanding of its audience's wants and, even more importantly, *needs*.

> ## Words of Wisdom
>
> *If you're not authentic, it's hard to get people to show up and stick around.*
>
> —Gina Bianchini, CEO, Ning

There are several things to consider before you even start to build your community. First of all, as you decide what kind of community to form, consider targeting a community or group of which you are already a part or an interest you already have.

Suppose you make pottery as a hobby (or even as a business) and you travel around to different craft shows and festivals to exhibit and/or sell your products. You will have met a lot of people at these events. You may even have a mailing list of customers who purchased your products at one of the venues or an e-mail list to keep in contact with your clients and other craftspeople. In fact, you might even have a website displaying your products. Imagine how easy it would be to take this to the next level: an online network made up of people who 1) love to make pottery and 2) love to buy handmade pottery. You already have knowledge of the product, and you already have a presence from the connections you have already made.

Why is building a community quickly so important? A lot of it viral marketing: You have to get your members to talk to (or e-mail) others about your network on your behalf.

CLICK TIP

It is much easier to create a network with a theme you already know and with which you are at least somewhat involved. You also have a much better chance of building your network quickly if you build it for an existing network of people with a common interest.

The "Buzz" Factor

When Google launched its free e-mail service Gmail, it initially opened only to a small group of "beta testers" who, in turn, were given a limited number of invitations that they could send to others via e-mail. This gave the program an air of exclusivity that added to the "buzz" about the new service. Sometimes, exclusive works . . . you have to decide it will work for you.

Planning Your Community: Open vs. Gated

It is important to decide whether to build an "open" (anyone can join) or a "gated" (must be invited by member to join) site from the very beginning, as it will have a strong influence on how you can make money from your network. Most of the software packages you use will allow you to modify your policy at a later date, but you should consider the options carefully when planning your community.

For example, we created a network to test a software platform (see Chapter 5). Although the target audience was in a specific geographic region, we did not limit membership to that area, and decided to make it an open community.

However, we could have built a gated community, giving members the option to invite (or approve) other members. Or we could have allowed members the option of deciding who would have full or partial access to their profiles, pages, or other areas.

You may set other criteria altogether. In their book *The Virtual Handshake*, authors Scott Allen and David Teten discuss an exclusive virtual community called the Value Investors Club (valueinvestorsclub.com). There is no fee to join, but you must meet strict requirements to become and remain a member.

Host of a Party for Thousands

It's important to design your site for several levels of participation. Every network will have its "core" members and those who seem to float around the periphery. Think of it like a party (an analogy aptly described by Gina Bianchini of Ning in her corporate blog): You need to be ready to provide a great event, with service, for your guests—whether they number 5 or 5,000!

(Ms. Bianchini was kind enough to allow us to feature her analogy here. To see the complete post go to: blog.ning.com/2007/03/eight_steps_to_creating _a_grea.html.)

Eight Steps to Creating a Great Social Network

1. *It all starts with a great idea and the host behind it.* Start by picking a passion, niche, theme, community, or topic you love. It's important to have a clear purpose—even if that purpose is just to hang out.

2. *Set the mood.* Let people know right away what your social network is about. Add a tagline and description for your network. The more specific, the better.

3. *Invite the right people to the pre-party.* It's always easiest to start with people you know. Successful social networks have all started small and have nurtured their early community. The first 50 members set the tone for any network. If you have friends with a shared interest, invite them and experiment.

4. *Spend time setting up.* Be a great host. Fill out your own profile page; add photos, videos, a couple of blog posts, and a few discussions that underscore what your network is about. It helps to have a unique point of view and way of describing things, although your members should be allowed to express themselves through their profiles in (almost) any way they'd like.

5. *Open the doors.* Once you've set the mood and have some early members; Link your new social network to your blog or website; Include your URL in your signature on blogs or discussion forums. Advertise on other websites geared toward the same interest.

6. *Kick it into high gear.* People want to be where the action is, so new discussions, posts, photos, and videos on your network are key, even if at the beginning you are the only one adding them. Come back to your new network often—ideally every few hours—and keep it going.

7. *Expect party crashers; then the police.* Expect spam, porn, hackers, and trolls on your new social network, especially as it gets popular. Like a

great host, it's your job to kick out guests who are out of line. Provide your members with an easy way to report spam or offensive material.

8. *Bask in the afterglow of creating something special.* With a good idea, a little planning, and a small amount of work, you can pull off just about anything, including your very own social network!

—Ning.com Blog (Gina Bianchini)

We have already covered the many features of a network, but remember that it's not enough to create a site full of hip and fun Web 2.0 features. You should make sure that all of those features support the overall environment of your community.

Never forget that your community may be designed and planned by you but it's built by the members who join and frequent it.

First-time visitors to your site will not be able to evaluate just what you are offering unless you have a clear idea and are able to communicate it clearly and quickly.

The main thing to remember is that you can't just launch your network and sit back to wait for it to grow. To succeed, your network will need to be designed around a great idea or concept, and as the owner of the network, you need to be the perfect host.

Chapter 4

A Small Fish in a Sea of Networks, and Why Bigger Is Not Always Better

*M*any experts, from social software developers to advertising gurus and those who study the new media industry, are discussing the Long Tail Trend in the context of online networks. Here's the concept: There are a relatively small number of "mega" networking communities (LinkedIn, MySpace, Facebook, Hi5, Bebo) that are extremely popular and attract millions of members; the majority of online (social) networks are much smaller and focus on single "niche" interests.

> ## Words of Wisdom
>
> *We are seeing the same thing with social networks. The smaller— more regional—ones are really driving the market.*
>
> –ALEXANDER GUTIN, PRESIDENT AND CO-FOUNDER,
> WEB SCRIBBLE SOLUTIONS

MySpace, Facebook, and LinkedIn might be names familiar to almost anyone, but many users (particularly those 40 and above) have found them too big and not targeted enough. There is, and will always be, a place for such sites, but niche networks are becoming more and more popular. It has also been said that the larger players would be even stronger if they allowed more focus on people's specific "niche" interests. One company that is capitalizing on that is online networking platform Ning, which will be of great help to you as you form your business.

In his book *Meatball Sundae* (published in late 2007 by Portfolio), author Seth Godin suggested that it is far more effective for an advertiser to reach a few thousand who *want* to hear its message than to reach several million who do not. And advertisers are starting to catch on to this—they will pay premium prices for targeted audiences. The social networking news site, Mashable (mashable.com) puts it like this:

> *If a company wants to market a $250,000 sports car, would it seem more worthwhile to entice the eyes of millions of heavily indebted undergraduates on Facebook? Or would it be better to seek clicks [pay-per-click, a form of internet advertising] from a smaller supply of people, such as ASmallWorld (asmallworld.com), the total membership of which runs around 300,000, many of whom are likely to be far more interested—and able—to make such a luxurious expense?*

On September 6, 2007, the *New York Times* ran an article about ASmallWorld, a by-invitation-only site calling it the "Facebook for the few." The members are (for the most part) very high net worth individuals. So it's easy to understand why a company like Remy Martin held a party for the elite members of ASmallWorld in late November 2007, and served its top-of-the-line, $1,800-a-bottle cognac at no charge throughout the event!

NICHE NETWORKS: A PRIMER

Typical characteristics of niche social networks:

- Focused around a specific topic, e.g., wine, travel, food, restaurants, home improvement, video gaming, anime, etc.

- Significantly smaller in membership than the general purpose social networks

- Extremely vocal members who are passionate and well educated about the topic that the social network covers

- Members are open to spending time and money on products that help them pursue their passion

Advantages of marketing to a niche social network:

- Provides highly targeted advertising to the consumers you want to reach

- Great way to seed a market with information on a new product or service. Passionate members of a community are likely to spread the word about your product to other potential consumers if they like it; you might have a grassroots campaign before you know it

- Often cheaper to run a campaign on a niche site than on the large, well known social networks

—From *Strategicast* (strategicast.com), written by Nikhil Nilakantan, President and CEO at Social Span Media LLC, a social media strategy and marketing consultancy

Networks with a Purpose

Scott Allen, author (with Jay T. Deragon, Margaret G. Orem, and Carter F. Smith) of *The Emergence of the Relationship Economy: The New Order of Things to*

Come, and (with David Teten) of *The Virtual Handshake: Opening Doors and Closing Deals Online,* is an expert in new media and social networking. He feels that a new trend will develop in the next two or three years: The basic online networks that simply provide basic content or community interaction space will give way to communities that actually help people to accomplish their goals, whatever those goals may be. He believes that people will flock to sites that offer more of what he calls "social *around* applications," as opposed to sites that are just social for social's sake. They will want to join and stay active on sites that have applications that help them embedded within the social or mere community aspects. eBay (ebay.com), Amazon (amazon.com), and Craigslist (craigslist.org) have been aware of this all along, but now that the technology has made it possible for virtually anyone to create a network, the opportunities for innovative entrepreneurs are boundless.

> ## Words of Wisdom
>
> *People feel a stronger bond to a place where the whole user experience is [based] around a whole commonality of purpose.*
>
> —SCOTT ALLEN, CO-AUTHOR, THE VIRTUAL HANDSHAKE AND THE EMERGENCE OF THE RELATIONSHIP ECONOMY: THE NEW ORDER OF THINGS TO COME

For example, a site called MyThings (mythings.com) provides a personal inventory system. Once you join, you can see who in the community has the same "stuff" you have, or you can look for things others have that you want to buy. Members make "gift" lists of things they want others to buy for them, and each item is linked through an affiliate program (which earns the members a commission when someone buys the product by clicking on the link from their page). There are also Google ads running on most of the pages, targeted to the types of products being shown on a particular page.

And that's just one example of many!

When Robin Wolaner formed the TeeBeeDee network for Baby Boomers (tbd.com), she used what she calls the concept of *purposeful networking.* She chose a large audience (25 million men and women), and is succeeding in winning over many who may not want to "hang out" with their teenage or college-age children on Facebook. She is also winning away some of the ad revenues that previously went virtually exclusively to the larger sites. She says, "You have to start [your networking] to serve a purpose for your users."

ONLINE NETWORKS THAT HAVE FOUND THEIR NICHE

Check out these other online networking businesses with a purpose:

- Yelp (yelp.com) "The fun and easy way to find, review, and talk about what's great—and not so great—in your area"

- Chowhound (chowhound.com) "For those who live to eat"

- Corkd (corkd.com) "The simple way to review and share wine"

- Migente (migente.com) "Connect with millions of Latinos today"

- Daily Strength (dailystrength.org) "Anonymous and free . . . the largest, most comprehensive health network of people sharing their advice, treatment experiences, and support"

- Dogster (dogster.com) "Dog freaks and computer geeks who want a canine sharing application that's truly gone to the dogs," also Catster (catster.com) "A Dogster for cat lovers . . . here, kitty kitty"

- Mama Source (mamasource.com) "Find the advice, referrals, and insight you need, in a supportive community of moms helping moms"

- Good Reads (goodreads.com) "It's what your friends are reading"

- Ravelry (ravelry.com) "A knit and crochet community" (A site so popular that there is a waiting list to join!)

- Chess (chess.com) "Aims to provide a safe and enjoyable environment where chess players of all skill levels can learn, contribute, play, build, chat, and share"

- MerchantCircle (merchantcircle.com) "Join the 475,000 businesses across the country who rely on MerchantCircle to manage their online reviews"

- My Venture Pad (myventurepad.com) "The online community for business owners and managers"

- Multiply (multiply.com) "The best way to share everything"

Another niche network, Where Are You Now (wayn.com) is an online network for international travelers. AT&T has promoted one of its global cell phones on the site. The community is made up almost entirely of members who would certainly have a use for such an item and the ad carries a lot more meaning here than it would as a more random placement in a larger network.

CareerCo (careerco.com—*still in development at the time of this writing*) is in the planning stages to be a job listing site built around an online network dedicated to 21st-century job seekers. It was founded by Ray Thompson, Edwin Dean, Kathleen Dean, and Hilary Thompson who had the idea for their unique concept after looking carefully at popular job-search sites. While they did certainly see some "networking" aspects in Monster.com and Careerbuilder, among others, these entrepreneurs decided that these sites' basic goals were to get as many job listings as possible and to deliver as many responses to those job listings as possible. At the end of the day, they decided, neither side—employer or employee—was being very well served.

To that end they started CareerCo, an innovative online job search and support platform for jobseekers and employers in the Denver Metro area initially, with plans to expand across the country. The company will offer a networking component to its jobseekers, where they can direct questions to other members who may have worked, or are working, for a particular company, so they can learn more about the company culture before deciding whether or not to apply. Jobseekers can post online profiles, which they can keep private, or allow everyone to access—including potential employers.

In the planning stages, the developers focused the site on a very narrow niche: Primarily women returning to the job market. They eventually expanded the site to focus on other special interest groups, such as the newest

---

CLICK TIP

Support and advice blogs can be big moneymakers. Form a great network that attracts people from a certain ethnicity, with a certain disease, or even a particular age group.

wave of employees entering the workforce: recent graduates. This group is much more interested in a good worklife balance than previous generations, and CareerCo is building entire resources for people with this goal.

Revenues from the site come not only from employer-paid job listings, but also from advertisements and premium member services, such as individual and group career and life coaching services.

Focused Markets Draw in the Ad Dollars

Networks are beginning to focus on smaller, more defined groups. If you choose to build a more focused community and get it to thrive, you will be able to command much higher ad revenues.

According to Bob Crull, founder of ONEsite, a social networking software platform, the networks that he has seen take off are those with a tight fan base, or built around an affinity group. One such group is Less Than Four (lessthanfour.org), a space for people who have suffered a limb amputation. A niche group with specific needs, and if you visit the site, you can see ads targeted directly to its audience.

CNN ran an AP story in early 2008, entitled "MySpace, Facebook: Big not always better." The feature gave a glowing report of the trend away from Facebook, MySpace or, as they put it, "any other online hangout that boasts tens or hundreds of millions of people." It went on to say that social networking sites that targeted people interested in a specific hobby, sport, or basically any specific interest are paving the way of the future. And these sites are reaping the benefits of having such focused, targeted audiences. According to the article, the online networking business Athlinks (athlinks.com) has built what it terms "the most comprehensive database of endurance race results anywhere in the world." Its membership is approximately 35,000, and it makes its revenues by selling upgraded packages to club owners and coaches (individual athletes pay nothing to join), targeted advertising, and an online store.

CLICK TIP

The bottom line: Advertisers will pay a lot more to target a smaller audience of members who are virtually guaranteed to be using the products or services that a particular company has to offer!

CLAIMING A BIGGER PIECE OF THE AD-DOLLAR PIE

Spending on social networking sites is expected to grow 75 percent over the next year, to $2.1 billion.

Smaller sites' share of that money is growing.

Of the $920 million spent in 2007 to advertise on social networks, 8.2 percent went to niche sites, up from 7 percent in 2006.

In 2008, niche sites' share of advertising revenues was forecasted to grow to 10 percent.

—eMarketer, a research firm tracking online advertising

Even though you can certainly find a specific interest "group" to join on virtually all of the big networks, many people find the sheer number of groups intimidating and like being able to connect closely in networks with a smaller following.

Gina Bianchini, CEO of Ning, compares LinkedIn to a stadium concert, calling it a wonderful means of reconnecting with colleagues you have lost track of, finding new people, or getting an incredible amount of new information as a result of having access to so many members. On the other hand, she compares smaller, more focused networks to an intimate dinner party comprised of like-minded people with the same general focus or interest in a particular subject.

Ning is certainly finding its place serving the latter—the company is helping users create millions of smaller networks with narrow channels.

Do you like what you hear so far? We'll end this chapter with a Niche Site Success Story: Dogster, Inc.'s advertising revenue doubled in 2007 from 2006, and more than doubled again in 2008! And check out a recent update from founder Ted Rheingold: "Dogster, Inc.'s 2009 revenue will match or beat 2008. Selling direct to a tight demographic is the way to go!"

Chapter 5

Software to Get You Going in Much Less than a Week

*N*ow that you've (hopefully) considered carefully what type of community you are going to create, it's time to get the technical tools to help you build it. As you decide, it's a good idea to look at what other successful networks use.

In addition to the online networks he has created for his conference attendees, Elliott Masie (see Chapter 3) has created a successful niche network called Learning Town (learning town.com) for people in training and learning. He has also built other networks "from scratch, twice." He has experimented with different software platforms, from the mass-market and simple to the more corporate (or enterprise) and complex. He reports that he receives e-mails about a new platform literally every day.

If you Google "online networking software," you will get more than 37,000,000 results (in .16 seconds); "social networking software" will narrow it down a bit—to a mere 24,600,000 results; "white label social network" will still yield over 286,000 results. It's incredible! Online networking is big business and growing every day.

As early as 2007, there were more than 80 companies offering "white" or "private" label social networking platforms, allowing entrepreneurs the opportunity to rebrand the application and make networks that are entirely their own. While the market is expected to become saturated, experts in the industry correctly projected there would be over 100 such companies or platforms by the end of 2008.

You will certainly have little difficulty *finding* software platforms. Choosing one, though? Well, that's where we come in—we've done a lot of the legwork for you!

Many of the platforms will not allow you to design and launch in a single week . . . but just as many allow you to get your site up and running in well under an hour! With all them, the more you want to customize, the longer it will take. You will want to look for a software package that will allow you to set up and operate quickly, but also to continuously add or embellish features as your company—and your community—grows.

One of the biggest misconceptions is that creating the actual online network is expensive. It's not. In fact, many of the growing numbers of networks that have gone live in the last couple of years were done on platforms that were completely free of charge. It is so easy to get up and running, it's almost unbelievable.

One of the best overviews we've seen of white label online networking software is in an online chart from Techcrunch, a blog recognized as a leader in "profiling and reviewing

CLICK TIP

For the purposes of getting your business up and running in a week, we suggest a software-as-a service fully hosted networking platform.

new internet products and companies." (See techcrunch.com/wp-content /white_label_social_networking_solutions_chart2.html.)

This list was built with the help of information supplied on Web-Strategist, a blog started by industry expert Jeremiah Owyang, now a senior analyst of Social Computing at Forrester Research. You can view his blog post at web-strategist.com/blog/2007/02/12/list-of-white-label-social-networking -platforms/. Originally written in February 2007, Jeremiah has kept this very important post updated regularly as the market changes. We highly recommend visiting the post early in your business planning—and revisiting it often.

The growth of online networking packages is reminiscent of the growth of blogging software: There are three (or so) very popular blogging packages, and several other somewhat-well-known packages, and literally hundreds of other tools for developing a blog, depending on your time, money, and staffing situation.

One of the main things you need to consider when you are choosing a platform is how much technical knowledge you have (or if you have a techie on staff, or even a sufficiently geeky friend or family member who could readily help you). Those with more technological resources may opt to purchase a licensed software package for online/social networking. But there are several software-as-a-service fully hosted service providers that allow you to set up your network unbelievably quickly and easily. For the purposes of getting your business up and running in a week, we suggest this option.

If your goal is to build an open network (as opposed to a gated or members-only network) based on a specific theme or interest, then one of your biggest success factors is building membership as quickly as possible. Of course, you will invite people to join in your initial marketing and promoting phase, but if you are doing this venture in a week, you might be best served by choosing a platform that, from its very design, will help lead people to your site.

Ning, Chinese for "peace," can offer just that. It has taken advantage of a concept

> ### CLICK TIP
> Don't reinvent the wheel! An entrepreneur just starting out will be better off choosing one of the many free or relatively inexpensive online networking software platforms.

CLICK TIP

If you are building your own site from scratch, you may want to consider "open-source" software solutions that allow you to easily add components to connect with broader social networking sites . . . but you will need to have (or hire) technical expertise to work with this option!

called the "viral expansion loop." This concept is based on the premise that if you set up an online network, you have no choice but to invite people to join it. In turn, those people will (hopefully) invite others to join (provided the network is something that appeals to the original invitees, which is why designing for your community is so important!). Ning has actually factored this into its plan for growth, and according to an April 1, 2008, article in *Fast Company*, one of the first publications to give a voice to this growing phenomenon of viral expansion loops, Ning has calculated that "each person signed up for [a network created by a Ning network developer] is worth, on average, two people." And this number is *compounded daily*, which has led to the incredible growth of Ning.

As we've mentioned, there are more than 100 companies offering online networking software or services, and the list is changing every day. The industry is still in its fledgling stages, and a single week can see companies leaving the market, new ones launching, and still others combining. For this reason, we will not provide extensive information on every company but will discuss in more detail five that are, for various reasons, excellent choices for starting an online networking business within the scope of this book. We have also provided a directory with URLs of some of the major players that have a product tailored to the solo entrepreneur or small business just entering the world of online networking.

Ning, "Social Networks for Everything"

Hosting by far the largest number of social networks on the internet, Ning offers virtually everything you could want for your social network and allows you to completely customize it according to your goals. The reason for this is that Ning offers its services on a platform. The best things about it are that a person with absolutely no experience can build an online network very quickly and have it look as sophisticated as anything a person with technical expertise would do. At the same time, it allows those with the inclination (and technical savvy) to build just about anything and run it through its platform. Learningtown.com, a social network mentioned previously in this book, is run on Ning.

CLICK TIP

A platform is software that makes services available to other software programs through Application Programming Interfaces (APIs). A platform, to computer people, is the software code on which third-party applications function, such as Microsoft Windows or Mac OS.

A California-based company, Ning was founded in February of 2007 by CEO Gina Bianchini (a former investment banker for Goldman Sachs) and Marc Andreessen (creator of Netscape). The number of networks on Ning has grown exponentially: In June 2007, there were 60,000 networks, growing to 80,000 in August of that year. At the beginning of 2008, the figure had grown to 150,000. In April 2008 it had over 210,000 networks on its platform, and as of June 5, that number had grown to over 300,000. Bianchini had at one point put the growth at approximately 1,000 every single day.

In the Ning Blog (see blog.ning.com), Bianchini posted a New Year 2009 entry entitled *Happy New Year, 700,000 Social Networks!* where she detailed even faster growth:

> *There is no question that 2008 has been good to us here at Ning. We ended the year with exactly 700,000 social networks used by millions of people in their daily lives. That's a 5x increase in social networks on the Ning Platform in a single year. More interestingly, 50 percent of these social networks are active, as defined as active usage by members in the past 30 days."*

> *According to the Ning website (ning.com), growth has surpassed even the founders' original expectations: "From artists to musicians, athletes, bloggers, video channels, journalists, students, educators, parents, craft hobbyists, alumni, and interest groups, the range and diversity of the social networks on Ning are profound.*

NING'S WIDE APPEAL

Age range of network creators: 13 to 75

International appeal: Members from 176 countries (the service is available in many languages)

Growth estimates by 2010: 4,000,000 online networks, "tens of millions of members," and daily page views in the billions.

Sources: Gina Bianchini and *Fast Company*

This means that, regardless of the theme of your network, you can likely find all the support you need either from the Ning support staff or information, or by joining Ning's own Network Creators network to get ideas and help from members of the network, because a wide variety of networks are already using Ning.

One of the things we especially loved about Ning is that it allows for individuality. Not just network owners but also network members can make their pages unique—they can design their own custom themes, even adding their own web designs if they are inclined and know HTML or CSS (web coding language).

The company has received a significant amount of press, particularly in technical and business publications, and has often been compared to Blogger (blogger.com), which made blogging available to virtually everyone in just a few clicks, for making online network setup equally as easy. It also offers a completely free package that is easy to set up (its home page is the sign-up page) and is a great starting point as you explore your options.

For research, we decided to create a network on the free Ning service. The network we wanted to build was specifically for dog owners in New York City, and so we titled it "Urban Dog." Within seconds, we had a domain name on Ning: urbandog.ning.com. It was so easy! We just had to pick a name and a web address for our network (see Figure 5.1). (There is a premium service that you can purchase so you can use your own domain name; see page 44.)

Figure 5.1: **NING'S SIMPLE NETWORK CREATOR**

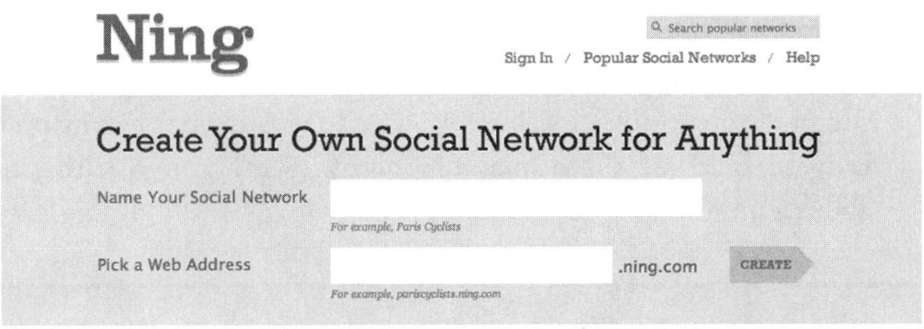

Ning·

Q Search popular networks

Sign In / Popular Social Networks / Help

Create Your Own Social Network for Anything

Name Your Social Network

For example, Paris Cyclists

Pick a Web Address

.ning.com   **CREATE**

For example, pariscyclists.ning.com

All in all, it took us about 30 minutes to set up our features:

➡ We set up Google analytics, a free service that tracks traffic and other activity on your site, and provides over 80 reports that are very helpful for your marketing and advertising campaign.

➡ We set up a blog and put up our first entry easily!

➡ We added a box with a Digg feed (see the box on page 42), which shows as a box of pet stories uploaded by people on sites all over the internet. It updates regularly (the jury is still out as far as the "cool factor" of this feature, as most of the links we are getting in the box are to photos and message boards rather than actual stories).

➡ We set up a badge (see Figure 5.2) to advertise our site on other large online networks such as MySpace, Facebook, and other well-known

Figure 5.2: **URBAN DOG BADGE**

networking, blogging, and promotional sites: Blogger, Friendster, iGoogle, Freewebs, Live.com, LiveJournal, Piczo, Netvibes, Tagged, TypePad, Vox, Xanga, Pageflakes, myYearbook, and PerfSpot. Ning created the widget for us, and we could customize the text.

➡ Then we set up a widget that would allow us to embed a photo slideshow on any other website we wanted to. Anyone clicking on our widget would see the display of photos. (See Figure 5.3; this took about a minute to set up!)

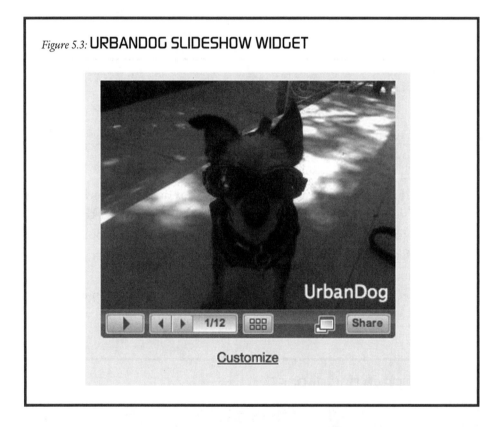

Figure 5.3: **URBANDOG SLIDESHOW WIDGET**

We added (courtesy of Google) a "Daily Dog Health Tip" box.

And—even though this was just a network created for research—thanks to Ning's easy-invite feature, we even added three new members in under an hour (see Figure 5.4)!

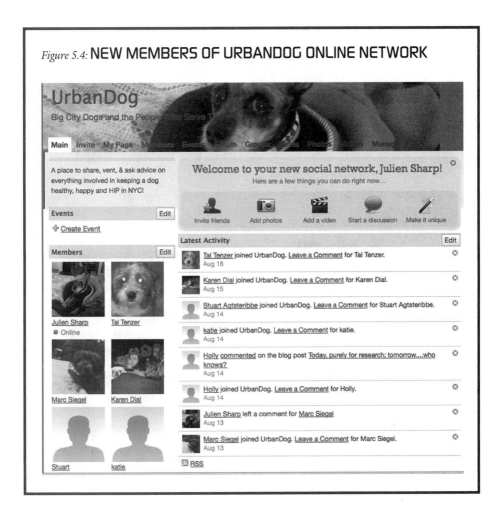

Figure 5.4: **NEW MEMBERS OF URBANDOG ONLINE NETWORK**

It was all so easy. Just a few clicks, and we had a full choice of features, including photo sharing, video sharing, and the ability to connect our members' photos to their Facebook profiles. Once we created our network, everything we needed to know was available in incredibly detailed instructions under the "manage" tab in our network.

Ning also has one of the best Help sections available without actually having to speak to a technical assistance employee. The Help page (help.ning.com/ is divided into sections: for members of networks, for network creators (this would be you), for developers. In August 2008, Ning did a

YOU'LL "DIG" DIGG

Digg is a place for people to discover and share content from anywhere on the web. From the biggest online destinations to the most obscure blog, Digg surfaces the best stuff as voted on by our users. You won't find editors at Digg—we're here to provide a place where people can collectively determine the value of content and we're changing the way people consume information online.

—digg.com/about

major upgrade to its Manage page (see Figure 5.5) where network creators are able to, well, *manage* the entire network. Other great features for what Ning calls its "Network Creators" can be found on its Resources page (see Figure 5.6).

Other enhancements include (per the Ning release notes):

➡ New appearance choices including transparency and better tiling options.

➡ Enhanced network themes with clearer separation between content areas.

➡ The ability to opt out of network invitations and messages without signing in.

Figure 5.5: **NING'S MANAGE PAGE**

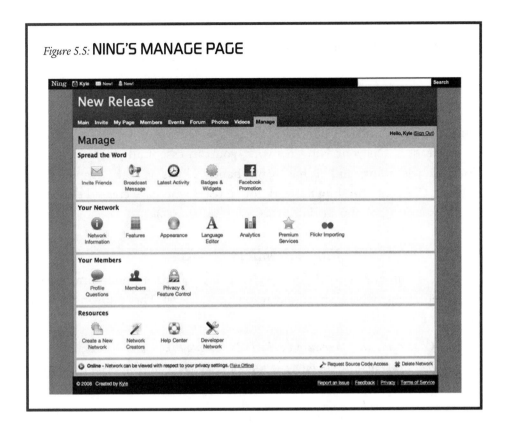

Figure 5.6: **NING'S RESOURCES PAGE**

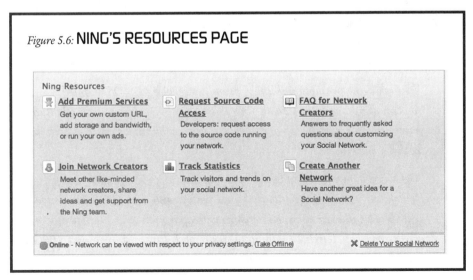

➡ The ability to approve groups.

➡ A few small performance enhancements.

Ning's "Notes" Feature

One of the cool features (of many) in the Ning platform is Notes, which allows you to do something very similar to wikis (a collection of web pages editable by any reader). On your Ning network, you can essentially create as many Notes as you want; and it has some handy Notes HTML templates on Network Creators, the Ning network for all users who have created their own networks—very cool, (networkcreators.ning.com/notes).

Ning's Premium Services

While we set up our network for free, Ning does offer four premium services for entrepreneurs who wish to take it to the next level. The following is from the Ning FAQ section:

"Control the ads" premium service ($24.95/month):
You can opt to run your own ads, using any ad server, or remove the ads entirely and use the right column of your network. If you do run your own ads, all revenue generated goes directly to you.

"Use your own domain name" premium service ($4.95/month):
Ning also allows you to map your own URL to your social network. And if your network's getting popular, you can purchase more storage and bandwidth instead of removing data.

"Remove Ning promotional links" premium service ($24.95/month):
You can also remove the Create Your Own Social Network button all visitors to your network see at the top of the page as well as the About this Network box in the right column.

"Get More Storage and Bandwidth" premium service ($9.95/month/unit):
By default, your social network comes with a quota of 10GB of storage and 100GB of bandwidth. This is a network with approximately 5,000 photos or 500 videos. You can purchase additional units of 10GB of storage and 100GB of bandwidth for $9.95 per month, per unit.

It's very easy to add any of these features at any time. Simply go to the Manage tab of your network (mentioned above), then go to Ning Resources to click on the Add Premium Services link; and the instructions will take you from there.

THERE'S NO SUCH THING AS A "TYPICAL" NING NETWORK

Networks using Ning "run the gamut" . . .

. . . from porn to Pez dispensers, motorcycles to motherhood, TV shows to customized cars to Thai kickboxing. Show My Pony is for horse enthusiasts, GAX for gamers, and GYNite for "gay guys and their friends." One of the most popular Ning networks belongs to hip-hop mogul 50 Cent.

—*Fast Company*, May 2008 issue

From artists to musicians, athletes, bloggers, video channels, journalists, students, educators, parents, craft hobbyists, alumni, and interest groups, the range and diversity of the social networks on Ning are profound.

—Ning website (ning.com)

Konnects, "Get Your Own Professional Space Online"

Very similar to Ning in ease of use but with a more "business" focus, Konnects was launched in 2006. The Washington-based company's goal, according to CEO Jim Crabbe, was to fill a gap in the market: to allow business professionals the means to connect to others all over the world by creating just a single profile.

Konnects allows entrepreneurs the opportunity to white label the entire site and be part of its overarching platform.

Konnects has put together a platform that is similar to Ning, but caters more exclusively to business professionals. In mid-2008, Konnects launched its second version, "Konnects 2.0":

> *The first thing you will notice when you visit Konnects 2.0 is the new Profile Wizard. The wizard will help you complete your profile step-by-step and guide you through the entire process. We have added a lot more ways that you can highlight yourself . . . from some of your personal interests like movies or activities, to a better way to highlight your education and work experience.*

Figure 5.7 highlights the features currently available for Konnects networks. There are two opportunities to make money quickly if you use Konnects for your network platform. If you charge members to join your network, Konnects will facilitate the payment process, and issue you a check on

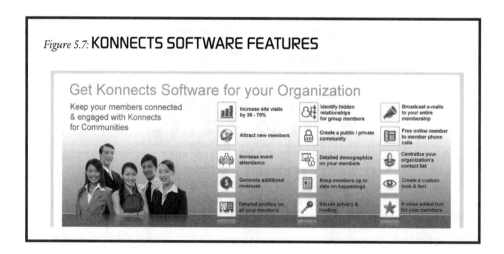

Figure 5.7: **KONNECTS SOFTWARE FEATURES**

a revenue-share agreement. You can also post ads on your network (paying Konnects a $19.95 monthly fee to opt out of their ads; if you want to build a network at no charge, Konnects will place ads that will appear on your site).

webNetwork™ by Web Scribble

Web Scribble, a company based in New York and founded in 2001 by twin brothers Alexander and Alexei Gutin, offers a very versatile and easy-to-use networking software package. As an example of the "youth factor" of this industry, the Gutin brothers were still in high school when they founded their company. In fact, they hired their first intern—a recent college graduate—before they had even started college themselves!

The first product the Gutins offered was a dating product. They saw a huge market for dating sites, but with a demand or interest in "smaller" regional sites to make it easier for people to find someone in their own geographic areas.

The brothers were doing freelance programming, and they kept seeing requests for programmers to build online dating sites. So rather than continue

WEB SCRIBBLE SOLUTIONS PRODUCT LISTINGS— TOOLS FOR ENTREPRENEURS

- *webNetwork*. Run your own web-based community or social network

- *webJobs*. A job board that lets seekers look for jobs and employers post them

- *webDate*. A complete software package that allows you to run your very own online dating website

- *webStore*. Allows you to sell photos, videos, music, or any digital product online

- *webClassifieds*. A classifieds site with unlimited levels of categories, billing support, and searching

- *webAffiliate*. An affiliate system that allows you to promote your site through others

to program for other companies on a freelance basis, they decided to make and sell their own software packages. The revenues from that initial product allowed them to develop new products. They closely followed online trends, and one that really stuck out was a need for software for online networking. They created webNetwork™. The demand for the product has steadily increased, and this year the company released its version 2.0 with even more features and enhancements. Figure 5.8 shows an example of a profile page, and Figures 5.9 and 5.10 show the software platform's search capabilities.

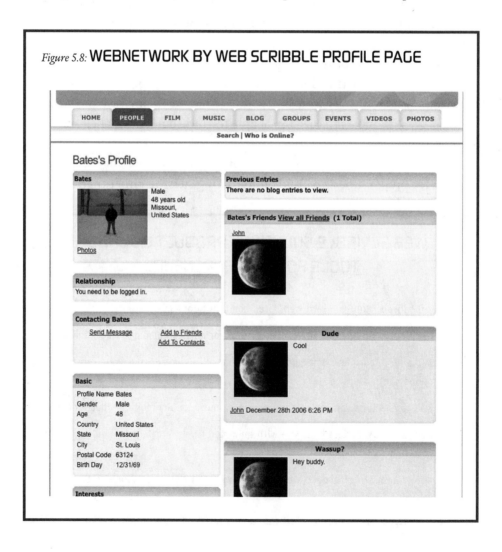

Figure 5.8: **WEBNETWORK BY WEB SCRIBBLE PROFILE PAGE**

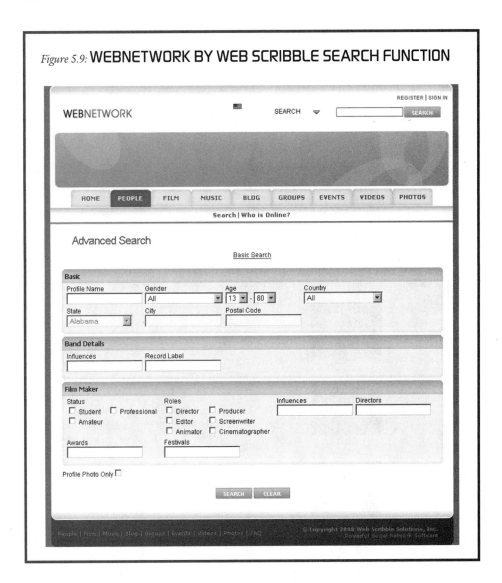

Figure 5.9: **WEBNETWORK BY WEB SCRIBBLE SEARCH FUNCTION**

While Web Scribble does compete in the social networking software market with Ning, the approach of the two companies is very different. First and foremost, unlike Ning software Web Scribble software can be run on any server.

Web Scribble charges $199 for the basic software and one year of product support, and additional fees for special features such as multilanguage support,

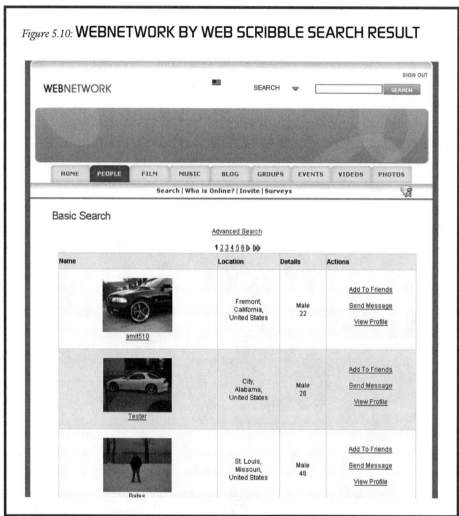

Figure 5.10: **WEBNETWORK BY WEB SCRIBBLE SEARCH RESULT**

live chat, live video (see Figure 5.11), zip code locator, and message board (forum) capability. Web Scribble charges for additional programming work, and also offers different monthly rates for support after the first year, with free upgrades for existing users. Web Scribble's appeal reaches to a large audience of customers, particularly small businesses or individuals.

Web Scribble provides what it terms the "starting point" for a client's website, and then can provide additional modules for a fee. When you first install

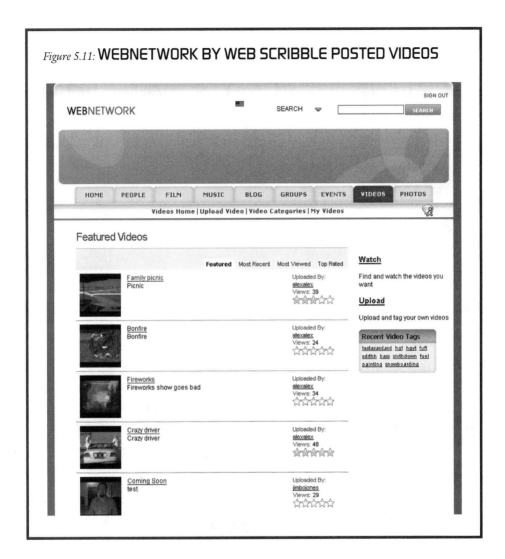

Figure 5.11: **WEBNETWORK BY WEB SCRIBBLE POSTED VIDEOS**

the Web Scribble software, you will have all the features that basic social sites have, and then you can work with a technical support team at the company to customize the software to your specific need.

Web Scribble has several clients who have purchased the software for professional networking and have simply modified the "pre-sets" to their own needs. For example, you could quite easily change the label "my favorite music" to "my profession" in the administrative area (see Figure 5.12).

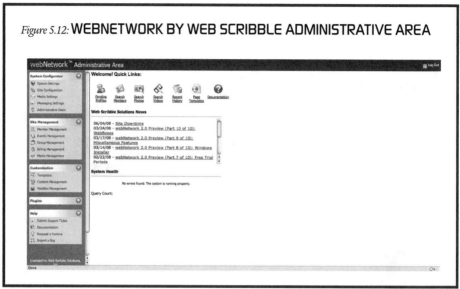

Figure 5.12: **WEBNETWORK BY WEB SCRIBBLE ADMINISTRATIVE AREA**

The goal of the Web Scribble team is for clients not to have to do any programming themselves.

You have the option with Web Scribble to run the software on your own server, but it also offers three hosting packages ranging form $9.99 to $29.99 per month. Hosting on the Web Scribble server is certainly the easier, more turnkey option. The price of the packages depends on the amount of space (storage), bandwidth (the amount of traffic transmitted from your site), and

WHAT IS A DATABASE?

Databases are essential tools for storing information that fits into logical categories. For example, say you wanted to store information on all the members of your network. To help store information related to each member, you could make a Members table that will store the following: Date Joined, Age, Gender, Profession. Databases are essential for storing whatever information you want to track, from the most basic to very detailed.

number of MySQL databases (MySQL is currently considered the most popular open source database server in existence).

ONEsite, "Industry Leading Social Network Software"

Known for its exceptional service, ONEsite is an Oklahoma-based company founded in September 2005; it is a subsidiary of Catalog.com, the first company to offer shared web hosting—almost 15 years ago! Like Web Scribble's product and unlike Ning's, ONEsite charges some initial fees to get started. The basic package is free (with the domain name transfer or registration), but other packages run the gamut up to the Custom Enterprise solution, which has a setup fee of $75,000+ and a monthly fee of $5,000 (see Figure 5.13).

ONEsite requires new users to either purchase a domain name through it (yearly fees vary depending on the availability of name chosen; the one we tried for demo purposes was $8.95/year) or to have a domain name already

Figure 5.13: **ONESITE PRODUCTS AND PRICING**

	Free	Revenue Share	Total Control	Radio & TV Station	Turnkey Enterprise	Custom Enterprise
Basics						
Setup Cost	Free w/Domain	None	None	$5,000	$50,000	$75,000+
Monthly Cost	Free	$49.95/mo	$199.95/mo	$1,000/mo	$2,500/mo	$5,000/mo
Advertising						
Your Advertising	ONEsite All	You Control Your Leaderboard	You Control	You Control	You Control	You Control
Tracking	None	Limited	Integrated	Integrated	Integrated	Integrated, Customized
ONEsite Advertising*	100%	300x250 Rectangle	None	300x250 Rectangle	Optional	Optional
Services						
Custom Design	Your Logo	Available	Available	Custom	Intensive	Intensive
Custom Development	None	None	None	Available	Available	Included
Managed Content Moderation	None	None	None	Available	Available	Available
Support	None	Available	Priority	Priority	Dedicated 24/7/365	Dedicated 24/7/365

NICHE NETWORKS BUILT ON THE ONESITE "DIY" PRODUCT

- *Hockeyscape.com*—everything and everyone hockey

- *Thecheerspace.com*—cheerleaders and cheerleading

- *Rcmate.org*—for remote control vehicle enthusiasts

- *Supdad.com*—for fathers

- *Myycatholicvillage.com*—for Catholics

- *Lessthanfour.org*—for amputees

- *Covenspace.com*—for pagans and witches

- *Enchantedfolk.com*—for enthusiasts of medieval fairs, clubs, etc.

registered to transfer to the ONEsite platform. This is very different from Ning, where anyone in the world, at any time, can register and build a network. ONEsite uses its registration requirements to weed out pornographic or other sites deemed to be offensive. ONEsite uses what it calls a Wizard to help with domain name suggestions (similar to the help you would find on Network Solutions, Dotster, GoDaddy, or other domain registration sites).

Clients of ONEsite have the following choices:

1. Launch on a new domain
2. Add a social network to an existing site (the company offers style sheets and smart templates that allow you to make your new network look exactly like your current website)
3. Move an existing site to ONEsite and add a social network

You could certainly set up a network with ONEsite in about an hour if you were on one of the two lower service plans.

Leverage Software, "People-Centric Social Networking Solutions for Business"

Though the primary focus of this book is to have an entrepreneur get an online networking business up and running quickly and inexpensively, we did want to highlight a software company that, though it would require more time and money to set up (certainly compared to Ning), has some amazing community-building features that you should know about.

Founded by Mike Walsh, CEO, in 2005, Leverage Software has an amazing people-centric software-as-a-service interface that makes it the vendor of choice not only for smaller businesses and startups, but for several large companies as well, including Reuters, P&G, Charles Schwab—even Apple and Microsoft!

As stated on the corporate website (leveragesoftware.com):

Leverage Software is the only people-centric social networking software on the market. We build every feature of our innovative suite of social networking products with people in mind, enabling our technology to connect you to the right person at the right time, whether that individual is a prospect, customer, partner, analyst, or employee. By creating relevant relationships with and among your target audiences, you enable individuals to grow relationships, share ideas, collaborate, and tell you exactly what's on their minds, which yields the information and insight necessary for business success.

With 60 percent of its customer base made up of small- or medium-sized companies, Leverage offers a lower price point than most other vendors and offers useful technologies to allow members to connect to each other.

One of the most interesting aspects of Leverage is its unique feature called a PeopleMap, which allows community members to identify other members who have similar interests.

In a recent interview, Mike Walsh explained the philosophy behind the Leverage product:

If it is important for customers to develop relationships with each other, our system is very good at that. Our product is designed to make it easy for our customers to find and talk to each other. For example, say we have two clients in the philanthropic industry, and they have some very specific questions of one another. Our software makes it very easy for them to find each other using a geographical pro-file and interests, etc. that help them to connect and develop those relationships.

If you have some startup capital to spend, we definitely recommend taking a look at Leverage Software. And if your business grows and you want to consider migrating to the Leverage platform in the future, the company can help move all of your profile data user discussions and other network information to its system.

It's So Easy

Just a very few years ago you would have had to be a programmer or hire one to set up an online network. Now you can do it for a few hundred dollars—and the price goes lower as more and more competing software packages come on the market! There are simply too many software choices available to cover each in detail. In addition to the five (Ning, Konnects, Web Scribble, ONEsite, and Leverage) we have covered in this chapter, below is a list of several vendors worth looking at for a business of the scope discussed in this book. We've included the product descriptions listed on their websites:

DatingPro Social Networking Software

datingpro.com/social

Our Social Networking Script Software can help you establish an online social networking presence within the shortest time possible and at a fraction of the cost it would take to develop your own in-house solution. Whether your web site is targeting the international market or a niche segment of this vast and expanding business sector, you will quickly appreciate the comprehensive features enclosed in this Social Networking Software and the flexibility provided by a template-driven solution.

AlstraSoft

alstrasoft.com/efriends.htm

Start a profitable social networking business by creating custom membership packages using Paypal payment gateway. In addition, we have added several new exciting features including online blog, forums, text-based chat, events and many more! Enhancements are also added to the admin backend and with our integrated banner ads system, you can earn extra income by publishing paid banner ads on your E-Friends site.

Dzoic: Handshakes Professional

dzoic.com

Powerful, fully customizable and feature-rich social networking software. Are you looking for an ideal software solution so you can start your own social networking portal? If so, then you have just found what you were looking for.

SNAPP® (formerly Me.com)

snappville.com

SNAPP® is a powerful tool for anyone who wants to build their own social network! From hobbyists to small businesses and large enterprises we have a SNAPP solution for you! In partnership with Google, SNAPP® offers a 50 percent ad share revenue for your site.

FLOCK: A BROWSER OPTIMIZED FOR ONLINE NETWORKS

Thanks to the beauty of open-source software development, you have more than a few choices for the tools you use to browse—and work in—the internet. Flock is a very nifty internet browser powered by Mozilla (the Firefox browser also runs on Mozilla). What is cool about Flock (flock.com) is that it has features that integrate with the big names in social media (Gmail, Yahoo!, Picasa, Facebook, Twitter, Flickr, Photobucket, YouTube, Blogger, and more). This allows you to find and contact connections across multiple networks, stay connected with what is going on in your networks no matter where you are browsing at the time, and get real-time updates of content uploaded to the internet. Flock calls itself the best browser for "internet multi-taskers," which is what you will have to be to build and promote your network!

Small World Labs

smallworldlabs.com/

Small World Labs Platform is designed to provide a base foundation for businesses and organizations looking to grow or establish a community. This foundation includes core features such as friends, forums, private e-mail, photo gallery, video gallery, and profile based participation. Online social networks can add additional interactive functionality to the existing website of a membership organization, association, club, team, university, church, or school. If you don't already have a website, the Small World Labs Platform can also stand alone as your online presence.

A Final Note Before You Decide

The package you pick really depends on the size of your network. In the beginning you might not need as much space, but factors to consider include: how many visitors to your site (remember your members might be inviting other members to join), how many pictures your members may be uploading, how many videos. Another thing to remember is that in recent years the price of hosting has gone way down. This is great for small businesses—you can run a fairly high-traffic site for surprisingly little cost.

Chapter 6

Getting It Right the First Time

*O*ne of the reasons many startup networks fail is because people tend to build the site without necessarily *designing* it. The tools supplied by the software vendors covered in the last chapter certainly take the pain out of building your site, and with their WYSIWYG (What You See Is What You Get) tools, simple-to-use color palettes, and user-friendly interface, you can graphically design the look of your site quite easily. But the

> ## Words of Wisdom
>
> *No one wants to be part of a social network that is a ghost town.*
>
> —Elliott Masie, Creator of LearningTown
> (learningtown.com)

concept of site design has another element: Your members must want to stay and use your network. For this to happen, it has to be a comfortable—and fun—place to be.

Before you even go live, it is vital that you make sure all the "kinks" have been worked out. If something isn't working, either fix it (or ask your software provider to fix it), or keep it inactive until a later date. Launching with a feature that is not working or is "under construction" does not look professional.

Make sure you proofread all of your content carefully! And after your launch, remember that you should make frequent content updates (at least until you get a lot of members to do it for you by building their profiles and pages). Try different things to see which features or updates draw the most page views—and hopefully new sign-ups—to your community. A "new member spotlight" is a great way to get people to come and stay: Most people like to see themselves in a featured web page!

For your initial content, you need to consider what would be valuable to your target community—your network growth is going to stall very quickly without a specific reason for getting your members to keep coming back, hopefully bringing their friends with them.

No one likes to frequent a store that is empty most of the time. The same is true of an online network! People are influenced by what other people are doing and where other people are going, in the virtual world just as they are in the real world. If someone pops in to your network and sees a lot of activity—new members joining, a new blog post or two written by you or other members, maybe some great new photos to browse—the buzz of activity will hold their attention and make them want to stay awhile. But if

> ## CLICK TIP
>
> The initial view of your site should have lively content that is easy to read; use bullets, subheads, and spacing to enhance the look of your copy.

SUCCESSFUL ONLINE NETWORKS CONSTANTLY ENGAGE THEIR MEMBERS

Look what the LearningTown network does to keep members involved—*and keep its homepage active and updated!* Community members get regular e-mails like this:

A message to all members of LearningTown!

TO: LearningTown Members

What are the Skills needed for great Collaboration? What are the skills that our workers would have (or that we should help develop)? Can you add a few to this list? Go to the front page of LearningTown and add your thoughts:

learningtown.com

————

Visit LearningTown! at: learningtown.com

that person visits your site and sees no new activity or commentary added in the past three days, they're outta there.

This phenomenon has occurred with many blogs as they have evolved: the ones that are updated the most are the ones that people come back to more frequently. In fact, many solo bloggers add other regular contributors to their blogs to ensure that new content is added often enough to keep the readership happy.

Building Your Community While Building Your Bottom Line

Chapter 7

Setting Up Shop

*O*ne of the great things about starting an internet-based business is that it allows you to work from anywhere. You can start an online networking community from your home, from your office (although you might want to be careful about working too much on it during your day job time), or even from a Starbucks. How often have you sat down in a coffee shop only to see a group of people having a sales or business development meeting at the table just across from you? It is more than likely that several winning companies were started over a grandé mocha frappe with whipped cream.

SETTING UP SHOP: BASICS FOR YOUR OFFICE

If you have never set up an office before, don't worry. It's pretty basic. Below is a list of what you'll need to get going, whether you work from home or an outside office:

- Computer (laptop or desktop, new or at least updated to handle all the elements associated with a Web 2.0 business).

- Extended service warranty (for your computer, which is the main thing on which your business depends).

- Virus protection software.

- Backup drive (can be a physical drive or an internet-based backup; just make sure you have some kind of backup system in place).

- High-speed internet connection.

- Server (only necessary if you are hosting the software for your network yourself, which we don't recommend if you are just starting out).

- Surge protector (make sure all your electronics are plugged into it).

- Battery backup.

- Printer (or a scan-fax-print-copy all-in-one unit).

- Fax capabilities (yes, a bit archaic but a lot of the business world still relies on faxing. There are many "e-fax" software packages that do the trick, as long as you have a scanner.

- Office furniture (desk, chair, storage cabinets/shelves/boxes).

- General office "supplies."

Still, you will likely want to have some sort of place to call your "workspace," and you can easily set up shop in your home. In fact, now is a great time to start any sort of business that would shorten a commute—or eliminate it completely.

Equipping Your Office

In addition to some of the more obvious office supplies, you will be running a technically oriented business, and the early investment you make on your technology will certainly keep you ahead of the game.

Are you going to be PC or Mac? There are positives and negatives to each. Take the time to research which operating system is best for you. (Full disclosure: author is a Mac fan.) Whatever computer you choose, make sure it is fully up-to-date, with the latest version of whatever operating system it uses.

At least in the beginning stages of your business, the computer (or computers) will be the most expensive item(s) you need. (Remember, anything you buy for your business is a tax write-off.) Because your business is completely computer-based, make sure you get the best extended service warranty, one that provides immediate service or a replacement unit so that you don't have any downtime should your technology fail you.

Make sure you have a separate backup drive or virtual backup service, for example, iBackup, available at ibackup.com. This is particularly important if you host the network on your own servers, but even if you use one of

---

CLICK TIP

It's up to you to protect your files.

- Back up files *frequently*.

- Plug *all* your electronic equipment into a surge protector.

- Battery backups will become your new best friend.

- Don't forget virus protection software!

DON'T FORGET YOUR BUSINESS LICENSES!

Depending on where you live and where you set up your office, you will likely be required to have one (or all) of the following licenses before you open your doors for business:

- *Business (or occupational) license.* Note: You may not need this if you have no "traffic" to your office, which is usually the case for an internet-based business.

- *Home-business (or home office) permit.*

- *License for sale of goods.*

- *Sales and use tax permit.*

Also, don't forget to register your trade (business) name with the state before you open a merchant or business checking account! See Classifying Your Business later in this chapter.

---

the software-as-a-service providers discussed in Chapter 5, you will certainly want to keep a backup of all your data.

Planning for Startup Costs

Take at least one day of your week to list everything you will need to start your business. You are fortunate that you can have your online network up and running very quickly and at very little cost, but if you want to grow your business, you should keep in mind the following startup costs that you will probably have, at least in the first few weeks or months:

- Business-filing fees
- Initial advertising
- Initial supplies
- Internet connection fees

➡ Insurance

➡ Legal or professional fees

➡ Licenses or permits

➡ Office equipment—including all technological hardware

➡ Office furniture

➡ Renovations to create your home office (if any)

➡ Rent and utilities at your office (if not working from home)

➡ Salaries/wages—for yourself, employees, independent contractors

➡ Service fees for network service provider

➡ Software for the network

➡ Website design (if applicable)

➡ Other expenses particular to your business plan or goals

Keep track of all your startup costs—your business should pay these back to you at some point, as a part of monthly business income!

Don't Forget Your Operating Budget

You will want to summarize what you will have to spend each month on operating costs. The more comprehensive you can be during your planning stages, the better off you will be in the long run. Try to avoid being surprised later on by taking your time now! Expenses will include:

➡ Advertising

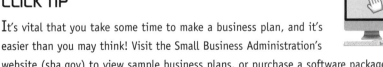

CLICK TIP

It's vital that you take some time to make a business plan, and it's easier than you may think! Visit the Small Business Administration's website (sba.gov) to view sample business plans, or purchase a software package to help you along. Business Plan Pro is an affordable and easy-to-use option (business planpro.com) although at this time this software will only run on PCs. Biz Plan Builder's 2008 version is pretty good, too, and is Mac compatible (jian.com/software/business-plan /macintosh-small-business-plan-mac.html#).

➡ Depreciation of your computer and office furniture

➡ Industry conferences (registration, lodging, travel)

➡ Insurance premiums

➡ Internet connection fees

➡ Legal or accounting fees

➡ Loan payments (if any)

➡ Maintenance or repairs

➡ Payback of a portion of your startup costs

➡ Percentage of rent or mortgage payments going toward your home office

➡ Percentage of your utility bills going toward your home office

➡ Professional membership fees

➡ Rent and utilities at your office (if not working from home)

➡ Salaries/wages

➡ Service fees for network service provider

➡ Supplies

➡ Taxes

➡ Travel (if applicable)

➡ Other expenses particular to your business plan or goals

Business Deductions

As a business owner, you are permitted by the IRS (and your state/local governments) to deduct all the money you spent on your business from the money on which you owe taxes.

We highly recommend that you set up a meeting with a CPA (Certified Public Accountant) before launching your business, especially if this is your first foray into entrepreneurship. While tax laws do change from year to year, below is a general list of the expenses you can deduct. These may not all apply to you, and there are certainly strict rules about the way deductions may be taken, which is why it is good to take at least one day of your week-to-launch to sit with your CPA and go over all the tax considerations for your new business.

Some of the more common deductible business expenses:

➡ Advertising/marketing/PR.

➡ Auto expenses. Using either the Actual or Cents-Per-Mile method—your choice.

➡ Business phone (and cell phone). Note: the business land line can only be deducted if you have a separate line from your regular (home) phone.

➡ Business related education. For example, you may want to take some marketing, general business, HTML, CSS, web, or graphic-design courses.

➡ Home office. You can deduct the percentage of the home used for business from all the expenses of your home. For example, if you use 15 percent of your home for a business, you can deduct 15 percent of the mortgage, utilities, insurance, etc.

➡ Legal and professional fees. These would include your CPA, lawyer, business consultant, advisors, and any other professionals who help you in your business.

➡ Meals and entertainment. Note that the IRS limits the deduction for these types of expenses to 50 percent of the total amount spent.

➡ Office/business supplies and materials

➡ Parking fees and tolls.

➡ Professional memberships.

➡ Subcontractors. If you hire independent contractors, such as designers, web programmers, or even freelance writers and editors, remember to report their income to the IRS as fees paid. Visit irs.gov for the appropriate forms.

If you are going to take business deductions, it is vital that you keep receipts or other records of all your expenses. For more information, please talk to your CPA, or visit irs.gov.

Classifying Your Business

If you form a business in the United States, you will need to define your business structure for tax purposes. You have several options, so it is good to consider the positives and negatives of each before making a decision. As with any business, it never hurts to consult with a CPA or business attorney, but here is some information to get you started as you consider which classification is the best for your online networking business.

There are five classifications to choose from: You will want to choose the option that best fits your vision for your online networking business, at least in the short term.

Sole Proprietorship

This is a business owned by a single person and is not incorporated. It is also the most inexpensive and the easiest to set up—you save having to pay legal and state filing fees. Filing your taxes is also easy: just attach a Schedule C (profit or loss form) to your regular 1040 income tax return.

If you are working from home, or at least do not plan to hire anyone to work for you, and are not partnering up with anyone, this is the best option for you. Just remember that you have the personal responsibility for all the liability (or debts) of your business. Also, a sole proprietorship cannot be passed to someone else upon your death.

Partnership

The main difference between a partnership and a sole proprietorship is that there is more than one owner of the business. In a partnership you will be able to share resources and experience; and it certainly can ease the burden of coming up with all of the startup capital by yourself! Another thing to consider is the benefit of partnering up with someone who has a different skill set or area of expertise. For example, you might be great at the techie aspects of your online networking business, but terrible at sales and marketing. You could partner up with a sales whiz, who may not be so tech-savvy, and skyrocket to success!

Another benefit is that two people can usually handle more work than a solo-preneur—think of it as a "whole is greater than the sum of its parts" kind of thing—and the business can continue even if one partner dies.

But, as with all the options, you need to consider the fine print. First, each partner

CLICK TIP

You can alleviate a lot of the risk associated with a partnership by simply preparing a partnership agreement.

shares the liability for all losses or debts incurred. You are also each responsible for the actions taken by the other. And the tax requirements are more complicated (you have to file the Partnership Information Return, Form 1065).

Make sure you consider these things and be diligent before choosing to take on a partner.

C Corporations

A "traditional" corporation is the C corporation. This type of business is its own legal entity. As such, the corporation files its own tax return and is "responsible" for its debts.

There are some clear advantages to forming corporation: In the case of bankruptcy, your personal assets are protected (only the corporation's assets must be sold to cover the debts). You are also protected from any lawsuits brought against the corporation, even those concerning work done through the business. A corporation can be continued even after all of the original founders have died. There are also many tax advantages to forming a corporation.

The main disadvantage to this classification is that it costs much more to set up. The fees usually run between $1,000 and $3,000 including filing fees and costs for a lawyer and/or CPA. As a small-business owner, you might also struggle with the "double tax" issue: in a C-corp, you are taxed twice—once as corporate income tax, and again on owner dividends.

WHERE TO GO FOR MORE INFORMATION:

SCORE (originally an acronym for Service Corps of Retired Executives, now known as "Counselors to America's Small Business"). SCORE is a nonprofit association dedicated to educating entrepreneurs and helping in the formation, growth, and success of small businesses nationwide: score.org.

Even better, SCORE is a resource partner with the U.S. Small Business Administration (SBA): sba.gov.

S Corporations

An S corporation is also known as a "small business corporation." It allows for the profits and losses to pass through directly to you (and the other owners, if there are any). This means that the profits are taxed only once, and the losses can be used to offset any other income you may have.

If you want to incorporate, this probably would be the best option for you, at least in the beginning.

Limited Liability Company (LLC)

The LLC is a distinct business entity that offers the same advantages of limited liability as a corporation but with more flexibility in structure, profit allocation, and taxation.

Your LLC can be taxed in different ways: If you are the only owner of the company, you file your taxes the same way as a sole proprietorship, but the Schedule C would have the name of your LLC. LLCs with more than one owner are treated just like a partnership, with taxes filed on the Partnership Information Return (Form 1065). The owners are taxed on all profits of the LLC.

Or you may be taxed as a C corporation. You may want to do this to take advantage of the fact that the corporate income tax rates for the first $75,000 of corporate taxable income are lower than the individual income tax rates.

Advantages of an LLC:

➡ *Flexibility*. LLC owners can set up any type of organizational structure.
➡ *Limited liability*. As with a corporation, the LLC owner's liability is limited for the most part to the amount of money invested in the LLC.
➡ *Pass-through taxation*. Earnings of an LLC are taxed only once, just as with a sole proprietorship or partnership.

The main disadvantages include the additional initial paperwork and fees in setting up compared to a sole proprietorship or partnership.

More and more small businesses are going the LLC route; and it certainly could be the smartest choice for you because your business will certainly include some form of self-publishing. If you, or any of the members of your network, happen to post or publish something that someone else may consider libelous, you can protect yourself personally from liability by forming an LLC.

FREE HELP FROM THE IRS

If you are going to run your business from your home, here are some free pamphlets provided by the IRS. They are available online (or in print) and can be obtained from the IRS website (irs.gov).

- Accounting Periods and Methods (#538)

- Bankruptcy Tax Guide (#908)

- Business Expenses (#535)

- Business Use of Your Home (#587)

- Casualty, Disaster, and Theft Workbook (#584)

- Examination of Returns, Appeal Rights, and Claims for Refund (#556)

- Retirement Plans for Small Business (#560)

- Sales and Other Dispositions of Assets (#544)

- Self-Employment Tax (#533)

- Starting a Business and Keeping Records (#583)

- Tax Benefits for Work Related Education (#508)

- Tax Guide for Small Business (#334)

- Corporations (#542) and Partnerships (#541)

- For information on S Corporations: Instructions for Form 2553, and Instructions for Form 1120S.

- Travel, Entertainment, Gift, and Car Expenses (#463)

Chapter 8

Protecting Yourself and Your Business

*W*e know you have a lot to do to get your business up and running in a single week. However, because you don't have to spend much time on the technology setup—thanks to all the great software-as-a-service providers—spend a bit of your week educating yourself on the general legal and liability considerations of running an online networking business.

We tapped the expansive knowledge base of Kaiser Wahab, co-founder and partner at Manhattan-based law firm Wahab & Medenica, to give you a primer on these important issues. Wahab is a dedicated business attorney specializing in business contracts, intellectual property, emerging growth/venture capital, e-commerce, and entertainment law. He has lectured at a variety of universities and conferences, including Harvard Law, and has contributed to a variety of publications. Attorneys at his firm have assisted entrepreneurs, artists, and software manufacturers manage their businesses for success.

Wahab takes a special interest in the legal aspects of social networking, and has written and presented many lectures on the subject, not only to owners or managers of online networks, but also to the attorneys who may represent them. Recently, Wahab was a panelist for the *Social Networking and Advanced E-Commerce Issues CLE*, Lawline.com.

Kaiser Wahab is in the process of writing a book dedicated to all things legal for online networks and other websites. He kindly agreed to provide a primer on the subject for this book.

The Statutory Landscape Is VERY Favorable for Operators of Social Networking Sites

The social networking phenomenon has only recently begun to catch the eye of legislators. However, the intricate web of copyright, privacy, and other laws do apply in some fashion. In addition, there is an upcoming wave of patchwork of federal and state law that will have significant repercussions for social networking clients.

Whether you are doing just a blog or a complete online networking platform for your business, it's important to know about the "safe harbors" that can protect you. Because online networking is about what people say and do, many startup entrepreneurs worry that they may be held liable for something a member, user, or commenter may say on their site.

I tell clients and audiences at my lectures that they should be aware of two protections: one against defamation (whether libel, which is the written act of defamation, or slander, the oral act of defamation) and one against claims of copyright infringement.

1. Protection Against Defamation: Communications Decency Act (CDA)

As has been mentioned in this book, online networks are designed to facilitate online and offline communication. Especially with younger age groups, users are often caught in a tangle of "flame wars" or tawdry bickering over everything from sexual orientation to race relations. Undoubtedly, the character of users is maligned daily. Ordinarily, using newspapers or other publishers as a benchmark, network operators would face liability for such defamation. However, the statutory landscape is VERY favorable to SNS operators.

Section 230 of the Communication Decency Act addresses issues of online defamation. The CDA was passed in 1996 and immediately subjected to numerous constitutional challenges, but Section 230 survived unscathed. It states that "[n]o provider or user of an interactive computer service shall be treated as the publisher or speaker of any information provided by another information content provider." It also preempts any state law to the contrary. In other words, an internet intermediary [which you would be, as the owner of an online network] can allow others to post materials online and not be held liable for it. The key to Section 230 is that the material *must be posted by someone other than the internet intermediary* [as the owner of the site, "in the middle," between the person making the claim of defamation and the person who posted the content, you would be considered the internet intermediary].

The CDA is often the first line of defense against user misconduct and has been consistently—and successfully—employed. Its purpose is to protect freedom of speech. As far as online networks go, this act protects the owner or operator of the website/blog/online network from claims of defamation because of content that a member has posted completely on his or her own.

Whatever the content, you, as the site owner, are protected as long as you do not editorialize the content yourself; i.e., comment on the content, or hire people specifically to write the content.

For example, suppose you run an online network about jewelry design and your members are designers who post pictures about their designs and discuss different venues for selling their creations, etc. One day, in the discussion forums, a topic comes up about a particular craft fair in a southern region of the United States. On that topic, one of the members comments that the person running the fair is a "Klansman," a racist, hates all minorities, and posts other potentially damaging commentary. Another person comments that she loves diamonds, and that same commenter begins attacking her in the forum, saying that "blood diamonds" come from Africa, and calling her a racist . . . you get the picture.

As the hapless owner of the site you may be wringing your hands by now. Thanks to the CDA, you can breathe a bit easier. The CDA protects you from any backlash that may occur from members—including any complaint from the object of the written accusation himself. You did not incite the comments; you merely created the framework for conversation, which led to these comments.

The key point here: You are not *obligated* to do anything about the attacks. However, as the owner of the site, you are allowed to remove the offending comments, or even ban the person who made them, since he was detracting from the purpose of the site by furthering his own agenda.

The CDA is particularly friendly toward the site owner in terms of comments made by members of the network that may be considered a national security issue. For example, if a member on Facebook posts that he wants to kill a national leader or other prominent figure, it is the writer of the content who may be getting a visit from national security, not the owner of the site.

Another interesting site—and we use that word loosely—is JuicyCampus .com. This site is literally raging throughout college campuses in the United States. It is like an online version of the bathroom stall—with comments about students—particularly female—being the dominant topic in the "bulletin board" based online networking site. The user has to check a very brief agreement before entering the site (see Figure 8.1). In this agreement there is a link to the much more detailed Terms of Service (TOS) Agreement. [Definition: The TOS governs the user's relationship with the website; in this case, with the online networking site.] But once they click on the Enter link to "Give me the Juice!" that's it. Then they have full access to post upon post, detailing students' escapades—sexual and others—and many times will include phone numbers. It is completely over the top and the CDA protects the owners of this site—*even though the site was created to provoke users to say the most sensational stuff possible!*

Figure 8.1: JUICY CAMPUS SIMPLE SERVICE AGREEMENT

As the owner of an online networking business, you can't ask for much better protection than that!

2. Protection Against Copyright Infringement

The DMCA (Digital Millennium Copyright Act) is broad legislation meant to bring the United States into compliance with international treaty obligations and address digital-piracy issues. This is something you would be concerned about if, for example, one of your members or users posted some content that he or she did not have the right to post.

Here is a bit of historical background: During the 1990s, the introduction of digital format created an exponential growth in copyrighted content distributed over the internet.

As content distribution increased, so did digital piracy. Copyright owners lobbied Congress to provide them additional protection against digital piracy. Internet service providers (ISPs), however, also expressed a concern that this increase in content would impose copyright infringement liability upon them for the actions of their users.

Section 512(c) of the DMCA addresses hosted content such as websites, bulletin boards, and forums. [This can now be expanded to online networking sites, which utilize features such as these bulletin boards and forums.] It provides a "safe harbor" provision whereby a person alleging copyright infringement can contact a site's owner and demand that the allegedly infringing material be taken down. Once the site receives the notice, it must:

➡ Remove the allegedly infringing material

➡ Notify the alleged infringer that the material has been removed

➡ Forward any counter-notice from the alleged infringer to the complainant

➡ Replace the allegedly infringing material if the complainant has not filed a lawsuit within 10–14 days after receipt of counter-notice.

A classic example is with YouTube.com. Say one of the registered members of YouTube posted all of the episodes of *Diff'rent Strokes* for anyone to watch. Viacom is upset because it was in the process of packaging the series for DVD sale, and now anyone can watch the episodes for free on the internet!

Under the DMCA, Viacom cannot just sue YouTube. It has to notify YouTube and give the company time to take down the challenged content. If the user/account holder doesn't say anything about having his or her posted content taken down by YouTube, then that is the end of the issue. However, the original user/account holder has the right to challenge YouTube, saying that they have every right to put that content up there. The account holder may very well have a right to that content. YouTube can put the content back on the site, and it is up to Viacom to sue the *member*—not YouTube—for posting material protected under copyright.

If Viacom does not sue the user or member within a certain amount of time designated by the DMCA, then YouTube—and the member—are in the clear.

This entire process must closely follow the process as outlined in Section 512. Even the content of the notice requirement is spelled out and must be followed closely, in order to be deemed "adequate notice."

In the unlikely event that this happens to you, it is helpful to consult with a lawyer. Also, as a basic means of protection, it is good practice to outline these requirements in a Terms of Service (TOS) section of your site.

When you write your TOS, you must also designate a copyright agent, and name them in the TOS. The copyright agent will receive all notices from complainants. This copyright agent (which would be you, if you are the sole owner/operator of your online networking site) must be registered with the U.S. Copyright Office, which costs just a $30 fee.

It's important to note that the safe harbor provisions of Section 512 are *not* available to site operators who:

1. Know about the infringing activity and do nothing about it, or
2. Receive a financial benefit from it

Privacy Issues

In addition to defamation and copyright infringement, as an owner of an online network, you should be at least aware of privacy issues. (If you are planning to start a site geared at children, you should be *very* familiar with these issues, or start working with a lawyer right from the start).

Privacy laws [at the time of the writing of this book] are very much in flux and there is currently a lot of concern in the industry about it.

One thing we find interesting is the disparity between users of different ages about what is considered "private" and what is not. Users, especially those in the younger set, have been known to disclose everything from personal tastes to home phone numbers. This is a treasure trove of searchable, persistent data for a variety of interests, the two most obvious being marketers and cyber thieves.

The public concern over online privacy is fast becoming one of the fiercest battlegrounds in the social networking sphere. In my opinion, people will eventually just expect that everyone will know everything about them.

In addition to blog posts and comments in a discussion forum or bulletin boards, User-Generated Content (UGC) also includes the profiles that each user makes when signing up to join to the network. These postings do not disappear into the ether. They are persistent and are recorded in transcripts, postings, search records and a variety of other formats that permit all manner of data processing and mining.

Since online networking, by definition, encourages the disclosure of personal and potentially sensitive information, you should be very clear in your business plan how such information is used and collected—and you should make this clear to your members.

As an owner of an online networking business, you simply must be very careful not to disseminate the information about your users without their knowing it. Make sure you have a Privacy Agreement included in your TOC, which delineates what kind of information is collected from users and what your company plans to do with it.

You may be hesitant to add so many "legal-eze" links to your friendly site, but don't worry; most people don't read the terms, and your users are not going to be turned off by this. Just make agreeing to the terms part of your registration process, and whether they read the terms in full or not; you're protected!

The legal aspects of this industry may be daunting, but remember that the laws are in your favor as long as you have the basic agreements in place. In the long term, especially as the number of people on your site grows, you will want to speak with a lawyer who has kept up with the laws as they change, to make sure you stay protected.

—Kaiser Wahab, Wahab & Medenica LLC, wrlawfirm.com

Chapter 9

Promoting Your Network Creatively and Inexpensively

Once you have that million-dollar niche network site up and running, it's time to start driving traffic to it and watching the money roll in. But wait! You've only got pennies to spend on creating a web presence, and you're banking on this becoming a paid gig.

First rule of thumb: don't quit your day job just yet. There are lots of ways to promote your network, many of which do not require a huge outlay on your part but do take time, relationship-building, and investment in processes.

Identifying Your Audience

The underlying structure of successful online networks is a series of conversations between people who *care* about the issue you are promoting; people who really, passionately care. The first step in any sales promotion is to find out who your buyers are, and marketing an online network is no different. Think long and hard about the audience for your particular network and then get off your rump and do some actual market research by talking to your potential audience.

As we discussed in Chapter 4, your online networking business will certainly be more successful if it markets to a specific niche of users. The best way to start your research is to find out who else is doing what you are doing. Is there an existing network owner or blogger who might be willing to give up site statistics or user data? Can you read testimonials or posts on other, similar sites (or similarly structured sites) to learn more about your audience?

You should also think about where your audience is located, and go there to find them, physically and virtually. If your network targets small business owners in creative industries, try to attend industry events and networking groups where you can meet those people, hear their concerns, and hand out the link to your site.

Even large social networking sites like MySpace and Facebook serve specific markets. For instance, MySpace tends to attract individuals (mostly Gen Y and Z), bands, and artists. Facebook now has many businesses creating pages for their businesses. However, business users on Facebook are not allowed to use its search functions to link to other business or individual pages on the site, which means it may not be the most helpful avenue for building up your network. Still, an online business or network looking for one more cross-link could find this somewhat useful.

The large social networking sites like MySpace, Facebook, and LinkedIn are great places to build your web presence. While MySpace and Facebook were originally comprised of individual (primarily younger) members, this has changed drastically in the last couple of years. In minutes, you can create a page on each network about your own! Of course, these sites offer the capability for creating a profile specifically to talk about and link to your business. Although you are working to create similar networking opportunities on your own site and make them pay out for you, nothing says you can't build up your niche, connect with users who have similar interests, and find old and existing contacts while launching your site. Marketing your networks on other networks is perhaps one of the most user-friendly online business networking models out there. It's free, and these established sites can serve as great success models.

> ### Words of Wisdom
>
> *To give your site authority, "Identify key players in the relevant field and politely ask them to contribute [to your site]. Make sure to show them clearly that you appreciate their efforts, and to include those who're active in the field but don't have the same reputation as the before-mentioned key players. You'll help them get exposure, and they'll help you kick-starting your community."*
>
> —Peter Bihr, author of
> The Waving Cat Blog (thewavingcat.com)

You can also go online to find your audience members in chat rooms, on blogs, involved with trade journals, and writing in e-zines. These are relatively easy and free ways to learn more about the users you want to target. But if you have the budget to put some money into your market research, groups such as The Nielsen Company have launched online programs to track data about users and site traffic in a variety of industries. Nielsen//NetRatings (nielsen-netratings.com) offers tools for businesses of all sizes to define more clearly and scientifically their audiences.

Search Engine Optimization (SEO)

Almost everything you do to promote your site is geared toward search engine optimization (SEO). SEO is the new Holy Grail of advertising because, really and truly, if Google and other search engines can't find you, the people who have the money that you want won't be able to find you either. Even the world's largest corporations are beginning to put more funding in SEO and internet marketing because it appears to be the only form of

> ## CLICK TIP
>
> "Bot," "Web crawler," or "spider": A virtual robot (run by an intricate online software program) that searches the web for new and updated web pages. As the crawler finds pages, it places them in a central database, usually for the benefit of a search engine.

advertising providing a return on investment. This trend is reported in a variety of technology resources, trade articles, and economists' blogs, e.g., eMarketer (emarketer.com) is an industry market research firm that has identified this trend each economic quarter since 1996.

The idea of SEO is to do as many things as possible to get your site listed as highly as possible within search engine results on Google, Yahoo!, MSN, and others. Google is by far the most sophisticated and widely used, but if you follow the promoting guidelines in this chapter, you will get a higher profile across all search engine platforms.

One fast and easy way to boost your search engine ranking right away is to create a site map for your website. This works because it instantly makes your site more searchable by the major search engines' "bots" or "web crawlers." If you used a web hosting service with beginners' tools or free customer service to launch your site, it can often help you create and post a site map. Google also offers Web Master Tools, to which you can post your site map in various forms to make your site Google-friendly more quickly.

Search Engine Advertising

Advertising your site on a search engine page is generally the first thing that comes to mind when you think about how to get people clicking through to your page. Many large search engines offer advertising schemes whereby you pay only for traffic actually received at your site. However, search engine advertising can be an expensive and imprecise endeavor if it is your exclusive source for large amounts of site traffic.

Search engine advertising is used extensively by businesses of all shapes and sizes: large, small, web-based, office-based, and everything in between. Google AdWords is the largest system. You pay as people click your ad and are taken to your website (called the "click-through rate" of your advertising campaign), so you aren't required to pay unless the ad actually generates traffic to your site. Here is how it works:

➡ To get started, you'll create an AdWords account, including providing an e-mail address and putting a credit card on file.

➡ AdWords will then take you through creating one or more ad "campaigns." You will write a short headline and a two-line ad for your site, and set a monthly AdWords budget. For Google's program, this is the maximum amount you will be charged in a month for the "clicks" your ad gets. Other programs, however, like Yahoo!, might give a disclaimer that you can be charged up to 10 percent over this amount. They may also charge you by the day.

➡ After writing your ad, AdWords will ask you to create a list of keywords that relate to your ad, site, or services. Theoretically, when people search for these terms on Google, your ad will pop up on the right side of the Google search page.

➡ This is theoretical, because you have to be the top "bidder" for a keyword in order to be at the top of the list of ads (or on the list at all, in some cases). Some keywords are highly competitive and may be associated with thousands of other ads. Those companies with a larger

CLICK TIP

Impressions: An impression is the graphic representation of your ad on a search engine site, or the link to your ad on partner sites where search engines post ads. The higher your monthly budget for AdWords, for example, the greater the number of impressions you will have in all of the places Google advertises, because that budget means you are willing to pay for more clicks to your website.

monthly budget and those willing to pay the highest click-through rate will show up many more times than companies with a smaller budget.

However, you are still getting people to click to your site regardless of how many times your ad shows up, and you are also only paying for people who actually click through. You do not have to pay simply to display your ad as you would on television and in the newspaper, or in web banners, for that matter.

Still, if you have a very small advertising budget, there are other options. Search engine clicks are still quite general and may not be growing your target audience. Clicks to your site from Google and other large engines can sometimes be accidental, incomplete requests or come from competitors trying to drain your advertising budget, and it is difficult to track exactly how much business they really bring in.

It is important to point out that there are literally hundreds of search engines with advertising schemes. To "get out of the box," check out some of these:

- Adbrite—adbrite.com
- Adknowledge—adknowledge.com
- Bidvertiser—bidvertiser.com
- Clicksor—clicksor.com
- Customer Magnetism—customermagnetism.com
- Fastclick—fastclick.com
- iClimber—iclimber.com
- Performics—performics.com
- SearchFeed—searchfeed.com
- Value Click—valueclickmedia.com

Cross-Linking

The basic concept of cross-linking is that you want everyone you know and everyone who's ever thought about considering clicking on your site to have a reason to link to your site throughout their other online browsing. It is the way you bring content that you consider important to your site visitors (and search engines).

Looking at it from the context of other sites, links to your content from other sites (known as "inbound links) raise the sense of importance about your site. The beauty of new developments within Web 2.0 is that you have hundreds of creative, fun, and inexpensive ways to do this.

Viral linking is the most effective. Ning offers a number of useful features that help site owners create viral loops that lead, inevitably, back to the owners' Ning-based sites. For instance, users on a site created with Ning software can transfer badges, widgets, videos, and photos from a Ning site to other social networking sites virally, without having to paste any HTML code, as required by other platforms.

CLICK TIP

Cross-linking is Next-Gen, but it can't hurt to use simple recommendation services, too. Register with Recommend-It (recommend-it.com) and get your current users to send your site link to other colleagues in their networks.

Blogging also becomes viral when readers and posters link to your blog from their own pages on other sites. Again, creating engaging content that appeals to the deeply rooted concerns of your niche audience is the easiest way to make this happen. Alternatively, you can blog and post on other sites and link back to your own, or create a link to other blogs from your website.

Blog cross-linking generates more site traffic as users from other blogs click through to you in curiosity; and it also makes your website ever more search engine optimized. Aside from relevant keywords, outgoing and incoming links are the most efficient way to get your site ranked higher in search engine results.

CLICK TIP

Viral: Viral linking, distribution, loops, and other web elements are simply those that grow like a virus. They become virtually unstoppable once they are out of your hands because they replicate over and over as users link back to your site, link your site to others, paste your text and other HTML code and content to their social networking pages, etc. Your URL, content, and ideas begin to spread, just like a disease.

OPEN A FREE ACCOUNT WITH WEBLOGS.COM

"Weblogs.com, a VeriSign service, is a ping server that automatically notifies subscribers when new content is posted to a website or blog. Weblogs.com is the original ping service and receives millions of pings every day from blogs that configure their publishing software to notify Weblogs.com the moment content is published."

—weblogs.com

In fact, you should include the link to your new network URL everywhere possible online, including anywhere you blog, on your own social network page (such as MySpace or Facebook), and on any niche sites in which you participate (sites like Dogster and Catster offer space for pet owners to include limited biographical information). All this external networking will eventually expand the network of your site as cross-links grow and no longer require your maintenance.

Keywords/Tags and Tag Clouds

These elements may be the most important for drawing users to your site, keeping them busy networking there, making it easy for them to connect with each other and your content, and optimizing your site for search engines and cross-linking. In other words, they accomplish everything you want in terms of promoting your site!

"Keywords" and "tags" are virtually interchangeable as far as the purposes they serve and how they are used: they draw users to a site or other online element through labeling. They are generally always creator- or user-assigned. When discussing issues such as search engine optimization and generating user traffic for your site, optimization experts, techies, copywriters, or designers might urge you to include keywords or tags on your site to make it more search engine-friendly.

This means that when an MSN user searches for "online networking site," your site comes up in the results because that phrase is included somewhere in the HTML text of your site. (Note: Your startup site will have to be super optimized before such a general term draws it up in popular search engine results.) Composing web text that includes as many relevant keywords as possible will help drive traffic to your site.

Tags are also used like labels on dividers or file folders within your site. They "tag" information, blog entries, photos, videos, podcasts, links, and other elements so that they are searchable by users interested in those terms and related topics. For instance, Flickr is regarded as one of the first Web 2.0 sites to use extensive tagging for online photo databases. Multiple users are allowed to tag images with keywords that they consider relevant to a particular image, thus making those photos far more searchable (and find-able) for other users. The beauty of this system is that the Flickr creators get to sit back and watch millions of people, in essence, make their photos and databases almost infinitely search engine optimized, in addition to building an invaluable site database that requires no financial outlay or maintenance.

This could work similarly for your networking site. The more often users are allowed to tag elements of your site and increase their stake in your site—via posts to blogs and audio and video elements—the greater searchability the site will have for existing subscribers, new users, and search engines.

"Tag clouds" are the most recent module for embedding tags into the HTML text of your site. They are lists or graphic representations of keywords relevant to content on your site. More relevant tags or those that users search for more often are represented by a larger font size, or may be in bold, italic, or uniquely colored fonts.

Generally, these tags are not just words either. They are links to text or other content on your site and generate cross-linking. Let's suppose you have started a network for people who are into Burgundy wines. There would be a lot of "talk" on your site about different varietals of grapes going into the wines from that French region. A tag cloud of your site might look like the one in Figure 9.1.

However, be careful with tag clouds and keyword density, you want to avoid keyword spamming: posting lists of irrelevant keywords on your site in order to get users clicking to it as much as possible. For one thing, they might find it annoying if they keep running into your networking site for moms in

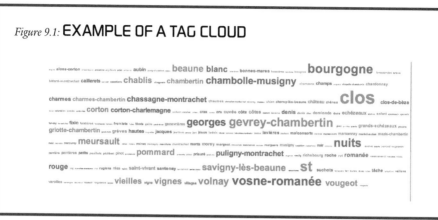

Figure 9.1: **EXAMPLE OF A TAG CLOUD**

small business when they're looking for the best trout fishing spots in Alaska. When they become moms who own small businesses, they may avoid using your overmarketed services. More importantly, however, many web crawlers, which scan the web continuously to update search engine databases, have built-in protocols for actually excluding sites that spam keywords. It makes their systems less efficient, so they don't want to include you in their search results. Tags should link to actual, relevant information on your site or the sites of your users. This is how you will best promote your site and create large amounts of lucrative site traffic.

Really Simple Syndication (RSS) Feeds

RSS Feeds are another excellent tool for providing incoming and outgoing links to your site, and you can also view them as a "public service" to your users. An RSS feed generally looks like a list of regularly updated headlines, called a "feed reader," that can be customized to display links to relevant news articles for your site users. Instead of browsing the web yourself, looking for articles and posting the links back to your site, an RSS feed will aggregate these links and post them directly to the site for you. Updates are automatic so that your feed constantly has the latest headline news related to your niche content.

You can also use the headlines and articles provided by an RSS feed to produce content for your site blog.

Invitations

Another great benefit of using all-in-one site-launching platforms like Ning or ONEsite is the ability to use "invite" or "share" features. These are simple modules that your users can employ to e-mail links to your site's content to friends, family, colleagues, networking groups, and other interested parties.

For example, at the most basic level you'll want your users to have the ability to send subscription invitations to their contacts, inviting them to join your networking site. This is a simple feature and has the potential to grow chain letter-style as second-, third-, and fourth-tier contacts get invitations.

However, it can also work for any content on your site. Users should be able to send links to interesting videos, photos, blog postings, and other features that their contacts will find of interest. And, if possible, they should be able to send them in a variety of formats: invite friends to subscribe to an RSS feed for updates, e-mail the link to a video clip on your site, "text to phone" a blog entry, and other multimedia functions.

Tracking What Works

It's important to keep data on your site traffic, user demographics, and the things that are working for you. There are a number of ways to do this, and all will make your life easier and your business more successful.

The first, and most important, is to track your site data. If you have a package from all-in-ones like Ning or Yahoo! Small Business Hosting, this may be as simple as activating a tracking program that is already part of your hosting account. Other hosting services such as Go Daddy, Register.com, DreamHost, and literally thousands more often offer little-advertised, free programs that you can access at any time to find out how many people have viewed your site, how many pages they looked at, how long they stayed, and in some cases, where they came from before and where they went after.

The most accessible and sophisticated data-tracking service available online, is absolutely free. Google Analytics is a free software program that will track the most minute web traffic information for you, if you create a Google Analytics account and paste its open-source code into each page of your website. (Note that Google Analytics also integrates with Google's ad sales software AdSense, discussed in the next chapter, and the two programs can work individually or together.) In order to appear as objective as possible, we approached an expert to find out why Google seems to have the best software for data tracking and pay-per-click advertising, and how it almost always manages to give it away for free. See the callout box on pages 102–106.

Ning also makes tracking traffic to your online network incredibly easy. On the second row of its Manage section (See Chapter 5), you will see a little bar graph icon with the title Analytics below it. Click on that and you will see the image in Figure 9.2. There is a box where you can paste HTML code to monitor the traffic to your site. (Don't worry—it's easy, as you'll see in the figure.)

All you have to do is open an account with Google Analytics (and Ning even provides the link to do that on the right of the page). After you do,

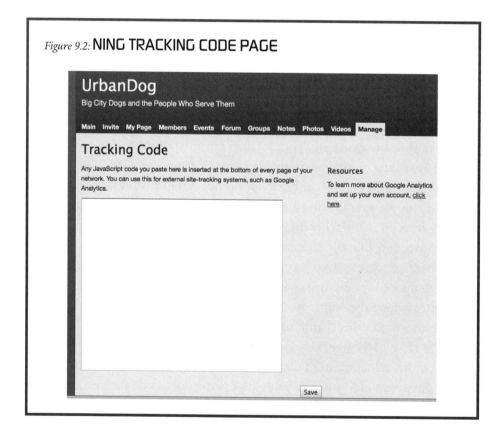

Figure 9.2: **NING TRACKING CODE PAGE**

UrbanDog
Big City Dogs and the People Who Serve Them

Main Invite My Page Members Events Forum Groups Notes Photos Videos Manage

Tracking Code

Any JavaScript code you paste here is inserted at the bottom of every page of your network. You can use this for external site-tracking systems, such as Google Analytics.

Resources

To learn more about Google Analytics and set up your own account, <u>click here</u>.

Save

Google Analytics will give you a few lines of HTML code, which you copy and paste into the large box under the title Tracking Code.

So, for our test network, we obtained and pasted our code into the box and hit Save. Then we sent out a lot of e-mails to friends, asking them to join our network. (Ning also makes that very easy, as you can easily upload e-mail addresses from your Mac Address Book, MS Outlook, or even from web-based e-mail clients like Hotmail, Yahoo!, Gmail, and more.)

Once we got a few people to visit our site—and a few kind souls to join for the sake of research—it was time to visit Google Analytics to see the action, which it had begun tracking for the site as soon as we hit the Save button!

Figure 9.3 shows in detail what information we were able to get about site visits after a *single day* of monitoring!

The first page of the report, also called the "Dashboard," shows some general statistics, including number of visits and page views, average number of pages clicked on per visit, bounce rate (how many people clicked away from the site after visiting the home page), how long people stayed on the site, and the percentage of people who came for the first time. Ours started out quite high, but happily, as we did more work on the network and added more members, the bounce rate started to decrease!

The second page of the report (shown in Figure 9.4) breaks down the visitors a bit more. It even shows what internet browser they were using to access your site and what type of connection speed they had!

If you are going to do any customization of your site, you will want to look at this information carefully (or have your web designer do so). Websites look different in different browsers, so you may want to optimize your site to the

BOUNCE RATES

This is a very important term to know: You have a "bounce" if someone comes to your home page and doesn't go anywhere else on the site. You want that number to be low, especially if you want to earn money from advertising, or if you want to "convert" a click into a sale of merchandise you offer on your site.

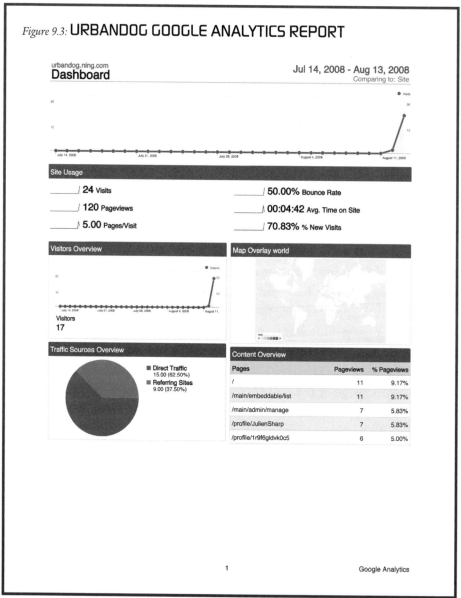

Figure 9.3: **URBANDOG GOOGLE ANALYTICS REPORT**

highest-used browsers of your visitors. The same goes for connection speed: If you see a lot of people accessing your site from slower-speed services, you might want to be careful how much bandwidth your site requires so that your regular users are not waiting a long time for data and media to download.

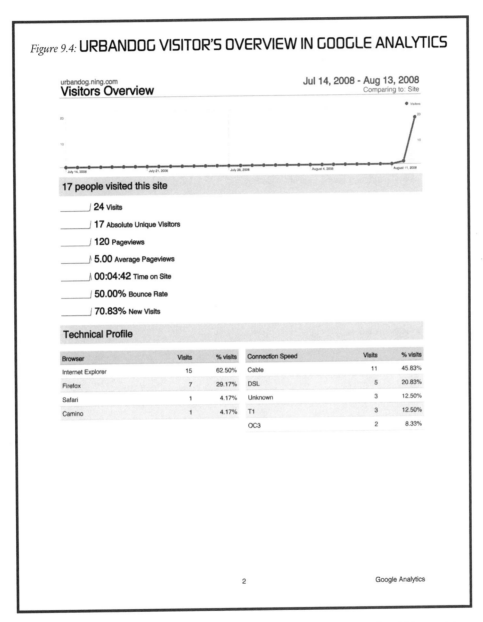

Figure 9.4: **URBANDOG VISITOR'S OVERVIEW IN GOOGLE ANALYTICS**

urbandog.ning.com
Visitors Overview

Jul 14, 2008 - Aug 13, 2008
Comparing to: Site

17 people visited this site

___/ **24** Visits

___/ **17** Absolute Unique Visitors

___/ **120** Pageviews

___/ **5.00** Average Pageviews

___/ **00:04:42** Time on Site

___/ **50.00%** Bounce Rate

___/ **70.83%** New Visits

Technical Profile

Browser	Visits	% visits
Internet Explorer	15	62.50%
Firefox	7	29.17%
Safari	1	4.17%
Camino	1	4.17%

Connection Speed	Visits	% visits
Cable	11	45.83%
DSL	5	20.83%
Unknown	3	12.50%
T1	3	12.50%
OC3	2	8.33%

2

Google Analytics

Figure 9.5 shows you how the traffic came to your site: Direct (they entered your URL or web address into their browser), Referring Site (they saw the link to your site from another one and clicked on it), or from Search Engines (Google, Yahoo!, etc.)

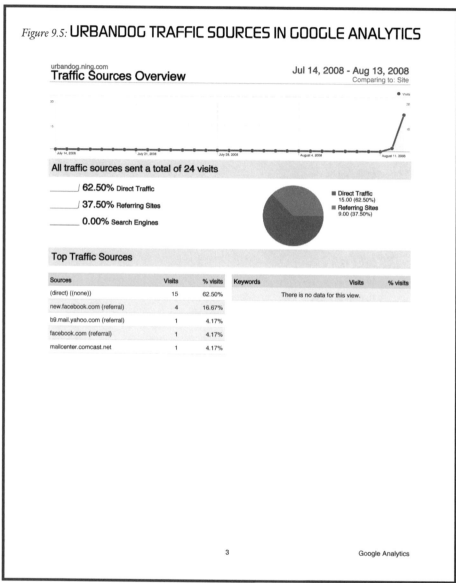

Figure 9.5: **URBANDOG TRAFFIC SOURCES IN GOOGLE ANALYTICS**

The fourth page is interesting, particularly as your site starts to get more traffic: It shows a world map, indicating from which countries people have visited your site (see our example in Figure 9.6). If you start to see a lot of hits from countries where English is not the predominant language, you may want to think about adding a site in that language.

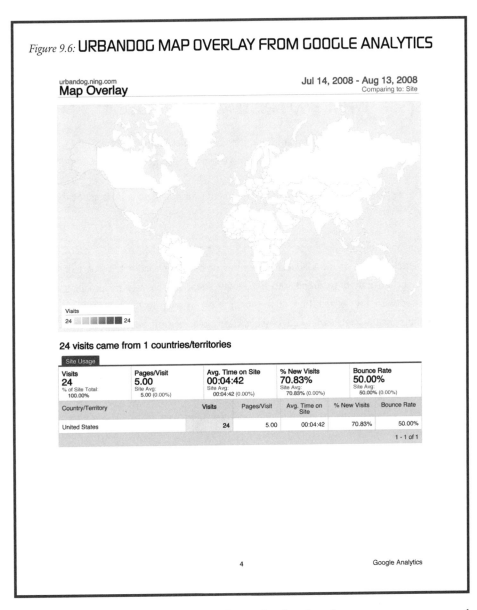

Figure 9.6: URBANDOG MAP OVERLAY FROM GOOGLE ANALYTICS

urbandog.ning.com
Map Overlay

Jul 14, 2008 - Aug 13, 2008
Comparing to: Site

Visits
24 ■ ■ ■ ■ ■ 24

24 visits came from 1 countries/territories

Site Usage

Visits	Pages/Visit	Avg. Time on Site	% New Visits	Bounce Rate
24 % of Site Total: 100.00%	**5.00** Site Avg: 5.00 (0.00%)	**00:04:42** Site Avg: 00:04:42 (0.00%)	**70.83%** Site Avg: 70.83% (0.00%)	**50.00%** Site Avg: 50.00% (0.00%)

Country/Territory	Visits	Pages/Visit	Avg. Time on Site	% New Visits	Bounce Rate
United States	24	5.00	00:04:42	70.83%	50.00%
					1 - 1 of 1

4   Google Analytics

Finally, on page 5, Google Analytics looks closely at your content, and you can see our content overview in Figure 9.7. It shows you which pages in your site got the most visits/pageviews. (The "/" sign means your home-page). As you analyze your results, you may see that one or two pages are getting a lot more hits than others; you can then try to figure out why and perhaps modify the content in your other pages to boost your results on those pages!

"WHAT'S SO GREAT ABOUT GOOGLE?"

An Interview with Paul Burani, owner of Clicksharp Marketing,
New York, New York (clicksharpmarketing.com)

Q. *There are a lot of companies making the same types of software as Google: Yahoo!, MSN, and smaller companies. Why aren't they used as widely?*

A. Generally speaking, Google's dominance boils down to the efficacy and scale of its search engine. It owns almost two-thirds of the search market, so part of this could be attributed to brand loyalty: people adopt complementary products and services with the expectation of a similar user experience. Google AdWords, for example, is a market-leading advertising platform because it automatically conveys access to that two-thirds' slice of the market. Alternative products, however, can still compete for two reasons. First, the non-Google market represents value, which remains on the table. Second, and more importantly as digital marketing continues to evolve, alternative products are often positioned to cater to a specific niche, which may represent a relative opportunity for businesses focused on a particular industry or market.

Q. *How did Google outstrip its competition in the search engine market to get where it is today?*

A. That's a question with many different answers. I tend to think it's a result of Google having democratized the medium of search, and to some degree, the internet at large. Its search technology revolves heavily around votes of confidence passed from one site to the next. Not surprisingly, end users have warmed up to the idea of exercising this voice . . . and inevitably they adopt other products and services in the process.

Q. *How is it that Google is able to offer its sophisticated software, such as Google Analytics, free to users?*

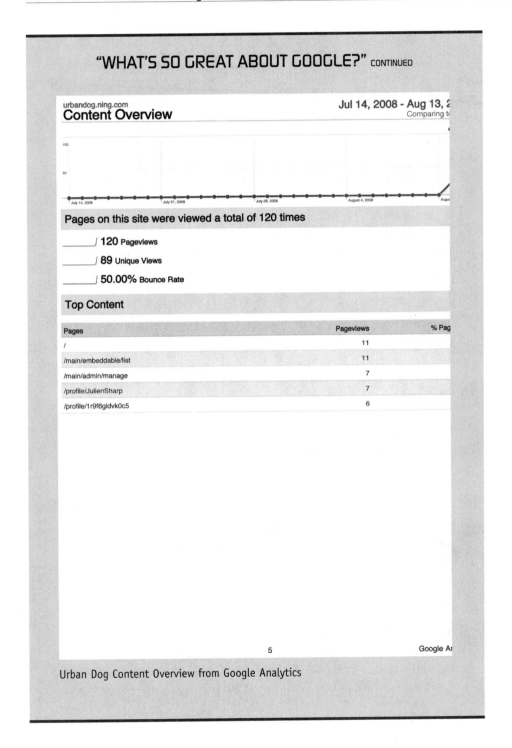

"WHAT'S SO GREAT ABOUT GOOGLE?" CONTINUED

urbandog.ning.com
Content Overview

Jul 14, 2008 - Aug 13, 2
Comparing t

Pages on this site were viewed a total of 120 times

_____/ **120** Pageviews

_____/ **89** Unique Views

_____/ **50.00%** Bounce Rate

Top Content

Pages	Pageviews	% Pag
/	11	
/main/embeddable/list	11	
/main/admin/manage	7	
/profile/JulienSharp	7	
/profile/1r9f6gldvk0c5	6	

5

Google A

Urban Dog Content Overview from Google Analytics

"WHAT'S SO GREAT ABOUT GOOGLE?" CONTINUED

A. The biggest reason is probably the high degree of integration between Google Analytics and Google AdWords. Google's engineers deserve a lot of credit for making the two products virtually symbiotic. Advertisers install the analytics software and see a wide range of metrics telling them a lot about their site, their visitors, their ad campaign performance, and how the three interact. Pretty soon they start to see patterns within each campaign, and are able to isolate the most profitable trends to their advantage. Their marketing return on investment (ROI) improves, their relative profits climb, their marketing budget grows. To keep the momentum, some of those profits are reinvested in AdWords, which explains how Google is able to finance the further research and development of such an amazing product . . . and offer it free to the public.

Again, this would be much harder to pull off if Google didn't have such a big share of the search [engine] market.

Q. *Are Google products at the top of your list for your client recommendations? If so, why?*

A. For pay-per-click (PPC) advertising and website analytics, Google's products are, indeed, the preferred software for most of Clicksharp's clients. We prefer AdWords because many of our clients are relatively new to the search engine marketing (SEM) game. Google is usually the quickest at getting results, and helps us with the reporting, which is so essential to maintaining the client relationship. Google Analytics is preferred because of the immense value it immediately conveys, and because it's free. It's nice to save our clients an extra line item on the invoice.

Q. *Do you think Google Analytics, for data tracking, is the best product available of its type?*

A. Actually, no. There are a few significant limitations to Google Analytics, which become very apparent with bigger, higher-trafficked websites. If you start generating long lists (e.g., referring websites, or unique keywords driving traffic), Google will limit the amount of data that can be seen at one time. It also stores everything on

"WHAT'S SO GREAT ABOUT GOOGLE?" CONTINUED

its server, meaning that it essentially retains ownership of all this valuable data. This is done for good reason: Google needs to ensure that it can manage the necessary bandwidth to maintain its product's functionality.

The bottom line is, if you're a Fortune 500 company with a vast website and millions of visitors, you'll probably want to look into a more professional solution. But the overwhelming majority of businesses simply don't have that kind of scope. Google offers its product to anyone whose website generates 5 million pageviews or less per month. If you're under that benchmark, you ought to be very happy with Google Analytics.

Q. *What type of user will get the most benefit from Google Analytics?*

A. Just about anyone with a website would be very interested to see metrics such as search engine keywords, referring sites, most popular content, and so on. If it's an e-commerce site and the owner leverages advanced features, they can up the ante by learning a lot more about their sales funnel.

Q. *What about AdWords?*

A. If the advertiser is looking for a one-size-fits-all solution, which is proven across a wide array of industries and offers immediate access to the largest possible audience, Google AdWords would be an intelligent first choice. Over time, I would always recommend experimenting on other platforms, provided there is an adequate budget to make it happen. Spreading oneself too thin across different platforms is a recipe for disaster.

Q. *What are the benefits of using the revenue-generating features of Google AdSense? Any drawbacks to allowing Google to advertise on your site?*

A. If you actively develop fresh web content, AdSense can be a very good way to monetize the traffic you're getting. That's why bloggers love this product. Google gives you a variety of ad formats, and you simply reserve some space on the page to

"WHAT'S SO GREAT ABOUT GOOGLE?" CONTINUED

show the ads. When visitors come to your site, Google matches the content they're reading to the ads created by its vast network of advertisers (including many people promoting on AdWords). Because the technology is so good at creating these well-targeted connections, people do actually click, and that's how you get paid.

It's important to consider, however, that hosting ads on your site immediately connotes a commercial agenda, so if you have any reason not to project this kind of image (a nonprofit organization, for example), don't take the decision lightly.

Q. *What's your best advice for promoting a new site?*

A. For starters, it needs to be a good site. Promotional efforts will fall by the wayside if the site is not written in clean, search-friendly code (HTML tends to work best), with engaging content and a high-usability interface.

Over time, it's important that the site remains active and dynamic; this will hold the interest of both your visitors and the search engines. SEO is an excellent long-term growth strategy, provided it is done ethically and sustainably. Never be afraid to invest in new content for your site; the payoffs can be tremendous.

Overall, the best advice is to remember that the internet did not reinvent the wheel: we're simply using a new vehicle to practice the same old rules of marketing.

Paul Burani is the owner of Clicksharp Marketing (clicksharpmarketing.com), a New York City-based digital marketing firm that helps entrepreneurs and small businesses promote themselves on the internet.

If you pay for search engine advertising, the search engine account will also give you exhaustive data on how many impressions your ad had within a certain time period (usually a week or a month), how many clicks it received, and which keywords got the most and least clicks. In addition, some services will offer suggestions about optimizing your ads and keywords to improve your results.

You can also register for a service that will track site statistics for you, including all kinds of traffic and user data. Some services you can look into include:

➡ ClickTracks—licktracks.com
➡ DeepMetrix—deepmetrix.com
➡ StatCounter—statcounter.com

SEO is a booming industry, and you'll find that a lot of companies exist to help you optimize your site. However, many of them also have excellent tools that you can utilize to see what kinds of keywords are the best in terms of SEO for your industry.

You can find out which keywords are ranked highest by different search engines for different industries, so that you can be sure to include them as tags and in tag clouds. Since this information is changing almost daily, the tools that SEO companies have created are a great time-saver for you. Check out www.seobook.com for an example.

Don't Forget About PR

Good old-fashioned public relations is something you should be doing from the minute you begin to form your business; and you certainly don't have to hire a high-priced PR agency to get the job done, at least while you are starting up. There are several ways in which you can take advantage of the internet to announce your business, and any milestones you have along the way.

First, you should be aware of a completely free service that is available on PR.com (pr.com). Here is an extract from its website:

PR.com is a unique website where companies can promote literally everything about their business in a one stop shop business marketplace. A cross between a public relations and advertising entity, PR.com is a directory of businesses, products and services, a press release distribution service, job search website, and online publication of articles, reviews and celebrity interviews. With a full company profile, each business listed on PR.com has a powerful means by which to generate quality leads as well as gain worldwide and local exposure for all of their products, services, and other business information.

Figure 9.7: PRICING OVERVIEW

STANDARD VISIBILITY	SOCIAL MEDIA VISIBILITY	SEO VISIBILITY	MEDIA VISIBILITY
▪ Your release on top sites like Yahoo! News and Google ▪ Permanent hosting on PRWeb.com ▪ Attach images and documents ▪ Track results with statistics on reads and impressions ▪ Two-day distribution	All the benefits of Standard Visibility, plus: ▪ Distribution on industry-specific Web sites and blogs ▪ Premium placement for enhanced search results ▪ Social bookmark links for increased distribution	All the benefits of Social Media Visibility, plus: ▪ Embedded news image ▪ SEO tools including anchor text for search optimized results ▪ 10 industry and 5 regional news feeds ▪ Advanced SEO statistics ▪ Next day distribution	SEO Visibility, plus: ▪ Guaranteed distribution through the Associated Press to top US newspapers and media outlets ▪ Add an embedded video to your press release ▪ Advanced analytics show you where your news is being read
$80.00	**$140.00**	**$200.00**	**$360.00**

Figure 9.8: PRWIRE DISTRIBUTION OVERVIEW

Distribution	Press Release Features	Reporting Features	Additional Services	
Distribution	**Standard Visibility**	**Social Media Visibility**	**SEO Visibility**	**Media Visibility**
Industry Targets	5	5	10	10
Regional Targets	2	3	5	5
Custom RSS Feeds	✓	✓	✓	✓
Made available to Google News	✓	✓	✓	✓
eMediaWire Distribution	✓	✓	✓	✓
PRWeb Page 2	✓	✓	✓	✓
Yahoo! News Distribution	✓	✓	✓	✓
Topix News Distribution	✓	✓	✓	✓
Opt-in Media Database		✓	✓	✓
PRWeb Page 1		✓	✓	✓
Pheedo Network Distribution		✓	✓	✓
Targeted Media Digests		1	1	2
Associated Press Distribution				✓

If you have a bigger budget, you may want to consider announcing the start of your online networking business on PRWire.com (prwire.com). This company describes itself as "a leader in online news and press release distribution, has been used by more than 40,000 organizations of all sizes to increase the visibility of their news, improve their search engine rankings and drive traffic to their [websites]."

As the owner of an internet-based business, you certainly want to make sure your business announcements get distributed in the best online media outlets. There are varying fees-per-release, depending on the level of coverage you are looking for. Take a look at the comparison charts in Figures 9.7 and 9.8. The fees are still very low considering the cost of hiring a professional firm on a monthly retainer basis.

There are also several books on how to be your own PR agent. We list a couple we found to be very helpful in the Resources section at the end of this book.

Final Thoughts

Here's an important point to remember as you consider the options detailed in this chapter: It's the nature of web-based businesses that the ways to promote your site will change constantly. Keep trying new things, and you'll find some that work and some that don't. Web 2.0, 2.1, and 2.2, and so on will continue coming up with new and exciting ways to help you make it work.

Chapter 10

Earning Revenue from Your Network

*A*s we've mentioned, the only way to grow your network is by identifying and identifying *with* your audience. Once you have a large, growing network, you will then have the capacity to generate multiple streams of revenue from your site. You'll not only be able to hit up your users for all kinds of monies and products to sell, but also sell to those users through advertising and marketing strategies.

You may have to try a number of strategies before finding the few that are really going to work for your enterprise. Remember that any online business these days is going to be in an extremely niche market. So trial and error comes with the territory, no matter how well you know your users and how good you are at doing your homework in terms of earning revenues. Just stick with it, remember that you had a great idea to start with and that your user base is committed to it, and hold on to the revenue schemes that work for you.

Subscriptions

An easy first step in generating revenue for your site, and one you can take from the very beginning, is to sell subscriptions. However, convincing people to pay for your services is another matter. You know that a lot of networking sites are already out there, and most don't charge fees simply for signing up. So formulate a clear subscription structure that will set you apart. You have several options:

If you have a very exclusive product for which you think people will subscribe up front, go ahead and give subscriptions a trial run. If they don't work, you can draw users back by using the premium plan described below or forego subscriptions for one of the other revenue-generating plans described further on. Speaking of trial runs, you can always offer a free trial with automatic enrollment after the trial period to test the workability of a subscription scheme.

You might also offer most services for free, with subscription fees for "premium" services, such as allowing users extra storage space for photos or video,

---

CLICK TIP

User accounts are also a good idea for security purposes. You will want to have a valid e-mail address for people posting information on your site so that you have the ability to regulate that information in case it becomes abusive or inappropriate in any way. You will then be able to deactivate the account and prevent that user from coming back. This is especially important if you plan on having a blog and allowing users to post comments.

---

or enabling them to remove advertising from their pages. See Dogster (dog ster.com) and Catster (catster.com) for good examples of this model. Another good example is LinkedIn (linkedin.com), which offers additional, fee-based services that allow users to search for other premium users, thus connecting directly with power networkers. Paying subscribers on LinkedIn are also given access to features that help connect them with other users in their field or fields of interest to them without needing an introduction through a known connection. Fees are paid monthly or annually at a discounted rate so that LinkedIn gets the money immediately.

Don't forget, whether you employ paid subscriptions or not, it is a good idea to gather at least some information from all your site users by requiring them to create an account. When networkers sign up to be a part of your site, you can garner valuable demographic information that will be useful for your future marketing. Further, users will certainly prefer to hand over demographic information rather than money, but it could bring you more revenue in the long run.

For instance, your networking clients may be loath to provide the specifics required to make a subscription payment online, such as credit card information, home address, full name, phone number, and other information they fear may be sold or used for even more nefarious purposes, like identity theft. However, folks familiar with the internet would generally agree that

---

CLICK TIP

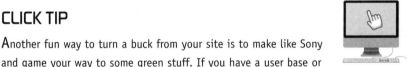

Another fun way to turn a buck from your site is to make like Sony and game your way to some green stuff. If you have a user base or content focus that lends itself to creating gaming features to which you can sell sub-scriptions, such features are often highly lucrative. Take a look at models like the iTunes app store (apple.com/itunes), which often shows that 60 percent or more of its most popular paid applications are games, despite many free productivity applications. Sites like Pogo (pogo.com) offer free basic games, with monthly or annual subscription fees for premium games ("Club Pogo").

---

they feel comfortable handing over their e-mail address, gender, age range, socio-economic information, and even zip code to a site with a reasonable privacy policy.

Aggregating this kind of information will not only help you better establish your niche audience in terms of generating content and promoting your site, but also it will be pure gold when you start pitching your site to advertisers and promoters looking for a targeted market. (The site traffic data that you've been collecting, as discussed in the previous chapter, won't hurt, either.)

Donations

Generally, you should not think of your users as a primary source of soliciting direct funds, especially without providing some of the premium services discussed above. You can typically generate a lot more revenue from allowing other entities to sell to your users or allowing users to sell to each other. However, in some cases donations might be appropriate, and they can give your site a financial boost if users are devoted enough to commit with money.

One thing to keep in mind is that networkers coming to your site on a regular basis will not want to be hit up for funds regularly. Remember that they are in this because they, themselves, want to grow an enterprise or endeavor, too. Sites such as Wikipedia have an invested user base committed to the goals of the site, so it sometimes runs a donation campaign, but generally

---

CLICK TIP

Hoping to make some operating capital from donations given by your members? This is where careful planning and development of your niche (see Chapters 4 and 12) and providing the ultimate in customer service (see Chapter 11) comes in. If you make your site a place to which people flock, and can't imagine missing a single day—or hour—of visiting and interacting, they will likely be happy to fill the "tip jar!"

---

only annually or biannually so users are not constantly "guilted" into paying for the communal service.

If you do decide to take donations, present the concept to your users as a temporary fundraising campaign, and give it a specific purpose (i.e., hiring a technical design company to create viral widgets and other viral software to help promote the site or funding more storage space for each member's site without raising subscription costs). This will engage your contributors' energy for the short haul and let them know that you're not counting on them to fund you on a regular basis.

You can also give the campaign momentum by designating a specific dollar amount as your goal, and putting a widget on the site to track fundraising progress. You can get these at sites such as democracyinaction.org, promotions.yahoo.com/giving, and conduit.com. You may also paste a link or button on your page that will take users to reliable sites like PayPal (paypal.com), Amazon Honor System (honorsystem.amazon.com), or Click & Pledge (clickandpledge.com), where the money will be collected for you.

Each site works differently, so read the terms and conditions carefully before signing up.

> ### CLICK TIP
>
>
>
> One thing to keep in mind is that PayPal, for instance, is not an insured bank, so if something happens to the PayPal system, your collected funds could disappear. You should regularly download PayPal funds to your business banking account. This also holds true if you have a PayPal account for merchandising. Before you commit to any of the sites mentioned here for fundraising, be sure to read the fine print!

Targeted Advertising on Your Site

The fastest way to get revenue coming into your site is to allow other sites and marketers to advertise on it, either through link advertising or with banners and flash ads. This generally means that as users scroll and click through your site pages, they will see graphic or link ads on the sides or at the bottom of the screen.

Since we used Google AdWords to talk about search engine advertising for your site, let's go through Google AdSense as an example of funded advertising *on* your site. Keep in mind that most of the big search engines will have similar programs for paying out revenues for the privilege of placing ads on your site. In addition, the company hosting your site may offer discounts on hosting or extra services if you allow it to advertise on your web space. Many independent partnering sites have also started popping up, such as Kanoodle (kanoodle.com) and SydiGO Networks (syndigonetworks.com).

In order to get an account with AdSense and similar advertising entities, you have to meet their requirements. In the case of Google, you must have a valid business name (so it can write a check to the business name on the account and you can cash it under that name), valid mailing address, working e-mail address, and finished website available for its inspection. Your website must also be in an approved language, and you must own the domain name under which it resides, with the right to publish HTML text on the site.

Once you have an account, you can choose one of two ad groups from AdSense to display on your page: either general Google advertisements or targeted ads. The first group are essentially random AdWords advertisements placed on your site by Google. The higher an AdWords subscriber's monthly budget, the more impressions it gets on "partner" sites, which is what your site becomes when you join AdSense. These random ads can offer any kind of product or service advertised on Google.

Alternatively, you can choose to have AdSense crawl your site for keywords and then pick ads targeted to your likely users. The benefit of this, according to AdSense, is that your site users end up clicking more ads and, thus, you generate more revenue. This is because, just like AdWords, it is the clicks that are paid for, not the impressions.

If you have aesthetic concerns, Google has an answer for that, too. Social network owners who have put a lot of time and effort into creating the graphic representation of their site may hesitate to clog it up with advertising, so AdSense allows you to choose how the ads look on your site. You can dictate that they appear in a variety of sizes, shapes, and locations on your site, and also choose whether they look like classified ads, graphics, or simple links.

For each user click-through to an ad, AdSense will pay you a portion of the AdWords user's bid price for that click (see the previous section on

"Promoting Your Site" for an explanation of this process). You may also be paid a portion of a large advertiser's flat rate (cost per thousand impressions on your site, or CPM). Regardless, Google pays AdSense subscribers on a monthly basis via electronic fund transfer, making this one of the easiest ways to generate revenue on your site.

Affiliate Programs

Affiliate ad campaigns are similar to services like AdSense in that they place graphic ads on your site, including banners and roll-over ads. Large online sellers like Amazon and eBay will start court-ing you for an affiliate campaign once you have significant site traffic they can take advantage of. Obviously, working with such big players can be extremely lucrative for your site. However, the catch in affiliate campaigns comes in the fact that you don't get paid for user clicks; click-throughs to the sales site have to result in an actual sale.

CLICK TIP

You can find more information on affiliate programs at associatepro-grams.com, myaffiliateprogram.com, and referit.com.

For this reason, affiliate campaigns will not be the most effective revenue generators for networking businesses. However, if your niche is specific to something that might be bought or sold on a large online auction or sales site, this method could be a goldmine. For instance, if your network is geared toward collectors of rare LPs or small businesses interested in buying bulk sec-ond-run books, ads from eBay or Amazon could pay serious dividends. Remember, again, that even if your niche fits with this kind of marketing, you will still need significant web traffic before it can pay off.

Branding Campaigns

Branding campaigns may be the most lucrative marketing scheme for bring-ing in revenue, but they also take the longest to cultivate because they require relationship-building with corporate sponsors. If you have grown your site's user base into a focused, niche market of people on whom you can provide

USER DEMOGRAPHICS YOU SHOULD INCLUDE FOR SPONSOR REFERENCE

Age Ranges; Gender Breakdown; Location; Household Income; Occupation; Time Spent Online; Number of Children in the Home; and Size of Household.

You will have been collecting much of this information already through subscription data, but you can also do a user poll or survey to fill in the holes if necessary.

data and statistics, you may well be able to arrange for long-term corporate sponsorship of your site, and guarantee its healthy growth and profitability in the foreseeable future. In short, you'll be set for life!

Once you have a generous market of site users and more-than-significant site traffic, you should organize the information about your endeavor into a package that can be pitched to potential sponsors. This should include detailed statistics on your user base, site traffic, revenues already coming into the site from advertising, and your vision of the partnership you want to form with the corporate sponsor.

You should spend significant time formulating this last element: your vision for partnering with a corporate sponsor. Once you've signed a contract for it to sponsor and advertise on your site, and agreed on how, when, and how much you'll get paid, there won't be any going back. First, consider your market, its needs, and the kind of products to which it is most likely to respond. You don't want to put a lot of time and effort into winning a sponsor just to have the campaign go south, along with any chance of a future relationship.

Also, do your homework before committing to having a large corporation pasted on every page of your site. If your network targets, for instance, green business owners, you'll only want to promote environmentally conscious companies.

Next, work out a reasonable and equitable way for you to get paid. The idea of sponsorship is that a corporation should be feeding money into your organization, regardless of whether users click on its ads or buy its products. However, it is likely that this scenario won't be acceptable to a corporate sponsor for very long. Write out how you are going to help promote your sponsor, what kind of timeline the commitment will work under, and the extended obligation after the initial trial period.

CLICK TIP

Elements of a pitch, in brief: User Demographics; Site Statistics; Company Financials; Current Marketing Profitability; Contract Proposal: Killer Presentation.

For instance, some corporate sponsorship programs work on a monthly basis, with a guaranteed CPM rate to be paid to the sponsoree. After the first month, the deal is reviewed and reworked. This will enable you to recruit multiple sponsors across months so that you have constant sponsorship without exhausting one advertiser on your market.

Finally, you will need to compile all your materials and generate a compelling, enthusiastic pitch presentation. The best person to present is you: the owner and founder of the networking site. Corporate officials will not want to deal with a middleman, and they will appreciate the ability to ask questions and gauge competency straight from the source. If necessary, you can employ a graphic designer, copywriter, or professional presentation writer to help you prepare the pitch, but in the end you should be the confident presenter.

Ad Federations

Ad federations are online groupings of smaller sites that come together in one place in order to be more attractive to large advertising clients than they could be individually. Ad federation sites like BlogHer (blogher.com, for women's businesses and blogs) and the Baby Center Parenting Federation (parentcenter .babycenter.com/babycenter-parenting-federation), affiliated with Federated Media Publishing, links to all of its member sites so that the combined site traffic for each is significantly larger. Each member site agrees to allow the advertisers chosen by the ad federation to advertise across the individual site. These ads are targeted to the demographics of users and members in the ad federation.

CLICK TIP

One way to make ad federations take a harder look at your application for enrollment is to boost your site traffic by joining them as a member site first, without applying for a piece of ad revenues. This will help you get a better idea of the market coming from the federation, in addition to building a relationship without a commitment on either side. It is also a free way to get more users on your site and build cross-links!

The ad federation itself generates revenue through advertising sales and membership subscriptions. In turn, member sites see their site traffic boosted and also receive a cut of the advertising revenues. However, there are generally application processes and qualifications to join and receive revenues. These may include site traffic requirements or content approval restrictions, and vary by federation.

Merchandising

If your site has a user community of business or social networkers committed to an issue that lends itself to branding, merchandising could be a two-pronged revenue-building source for you: you'll not only be able to put your logo or URL into the faces of your users' co-workers with nifty coffee mug merchandise but also put money back into your business fund.

Once you have a logo, image, or catchy tag line that you'd like to market, it's easy to take it to a printer to make up mugs, mousepads, T-shirts, and other items for you. However, before placing an order it's wise to do the math on how much the printing and materials are costing you, what kind of a reasonable mark-up you can put on the merchandise, and how much shipping and packaging will cost you, in addition to the time all of this will take from actually running your site.

If you can afford it at this point, you'll probably save more money in the long run by hiring a branding service (Cafepress.com is a widely used example). You basically hand over your logo and tell it what kind of products you

---

CLICK TIP

For more information on e-commerce, including setting up aspects of your site to represent a storefront, dealing with online shopping carts, merchant services, and many other e-commerce issues, reference *Design and Launch an Online E-Commerce Business in a Week* (Entrepreneur Press and Jason R. Rich, 2008).

---

want, and the service does everything else, including providing a web page that serves as a "store" from which your users buy the items. It also takes care of shipping, returns, and defective items. The downside, of course, is cost. By the time you pay the service, your profit margin may only be a few dollars. However, if you sell tons and tons of merchandise, you're still making some money to put back into the business, and promoting the business at the same time.

Thinking About a Loan

You want to give your business the best chance to succeed. If you are going to do this full time right from the start, you need to consider carefully how much you will need to cover all of your costs (including not only running your business but also supporting your regular bills and expenses). It is a widely-held expert opinion that a new business should have enough money to cover all costs involved for the first three to six months of operations. The time will vary according to how fast the business becomes profitable.

When you are putting together your business plan and estimating your operating budget (see Chapter 7), you should do a quick calculation: At the very least, you should multiply your estimate of monthly costs by three. That will give you a good idea of how much money you will need during the startup phase of your online networking business.

If you want to make a go of your business full time and don't have enough funds to start and run it right off the bat, then you may want to apply for a business loan.

TAKE A SECOND LOOK

Before you decide to apply for a loan, it's a good idea to look over your operating budget estimate one more time. See if you can lower any of the costs by holding off on purchases that are not absolutely essential to your startup.

If you are short on startup capital, there is nothing wrong with starting it on a part-time basis, while you earn money from a full- or part-time job. That's the beauty of starting an online networking business—you can easily start it in your spare time!

You can contact the Small Business Administration (sba.gov), which provides referrals to lenders that process SBA loans. You could also talk to a relative or a friend about a startup loan—they certainly may offer more palatable terms!

Venture Capital

Startup companies that needs funds for growth but do not qualify for loans because of debt may consider venture capital as an option. If you are a registered small business, you can look into a venture capital fund for investors. The upside is that these investors are generally looking to put money into high-risk, potentially high-yield firms like online businesses. The downside is that they usually expect to have a say in company decisions and to continue earning dividends if you become profitable. Most investment firms can give you more information about finding a venture capital fund. Here are a couple to get you started:

1. *Benchmark*. Generally considered to be the number-one venture capital firm, Benchmark funded heavies like eBay and 1-800-FLOWERS.com (benchmark.com).
2. *National Venture Capital Association*. This association has a website that will give you statistics on different venture capital organizations and help move you in the right direction based on industry (nvea.org).

A lot of tech company startups were launched with the help of an angel—an angel investor, that is. Angel investors are individual investors who seek out startup technology companies in which to invest in exchange for equity in the company. Unlike venture capitalists, they invest personal funds, rather than represent the pooled funds of others. Because they are private investors, they are generally able to consider smaller, high-growth enterprises—those enterprises that require a smaller beginning investment (usually less than U.S. $1 million)—than a venture capital fund can.

Online Networks: Run on the Internet, Driven by People

Chapter 11

Outstanding Customer Service: Let Your Members Be Your Guide

*T*here are certainly many things to consider in your busy week of designing and launching your online networking business. One of the fundamental things you will want to think of—if not in the short term then certainly once your business takes off—is how your are going to monitor your site. As your network community grows, it will be more and more difficult to keep track of the membership all by yourself.

You also want to make sure you have the resources to communicate with your members on a very regular basis. When you launch a new product or when you change something in the site operation, you should always tell your members why you are making these changes. If you are doing your job right, your membership will come to view your site as "home" and will want to understand the decision-making process . . . and perhaps even be a part of it on some level.

Community Manager: The Sooner the Better

At some point, you are going to need a community manager. This person does not have to be full time at first, and in many cases, you might not even have to pay them!

Brought in at the right time, a community manager can be very helpful. Before you launch, he or she can head the development and oversee the design of the community, as well as assist with writing and developing the initial content. But if you are launching in a week, you may want to consider hiring a manager after the site gets up and running. At that point the manager can monitor the site on a daily basis and moderate online forums and blog posts, as well as all other content being uploaded by the members. The manager can also encourage greater involvement by the members. Other useful tasks include: notifying the appropriate staff or vendors (or you) about technical glitches; or forwarding queries from members to the appropriate person who can provide a response, providing ongoing support to members about using the site, tracking site activity, and preparing reports.

> ### Words of Wisdom
>
> *We had a director of community before we actually had a community.*
>
> —Robin Wolaner, Founder, TeeBeeDee (tbd.com)

One of the most important things a community manager can do is maintain the security of the network. (The amount of work that has to be done in this area depends on the type of software package you choose.)

You may not have time personally to nurture your network, especially if it grows very quickly or you are doing this as a part-time venture. Don't despair.

However, you need not let your network run amok. You can "promote" some of the more active members of your community to help monitor the activities of the members and make sure everyone is clear on the rules and following the policies you have created for the community.

You can call these "power" members whatever you want. Some online network businesses call them "ambassadors" or "VIP" or "Elite" (see below). You can also give them advance access to information, such as new products or services you are launching, and ask them to spread that information to other

---

MEMBER MODERATORS: A SAVVY AND INEXPENSIVE WAY TO MONITOR YOUR COMMUNITY

Microsoft has a huge online community, and it rewards its power members with the title of MVP: Most Valuable Professional. From the Microsoft website: "Through their extensive community activity, MVPs help others solve problems and discover new capabilities, helping people get the maximum value from their technology."

The social networking site Fubar (fubar.com)—with nearly 2,000,000 registered members—has VIP members to help moderate the community and welcome new members.

Yelp (yelp.com), the location-based online review network community, has a group of premier members it calls the Yelp "Elite." The members of this group are expected to write a large number of reviews and serve as role models to other members. There are several requirements to becoming—and remaining—a member of this group, and there is a waiting list to join.

Learning Town (learningtown.com)—previously mentioned as a network for people in training and learning—has 42 members that have been appointed Mayors of the "town." They range from corporate trainers to directors of learning for companies such as Jet Blue and Disney.

---

members of the community. This can take a lot of the pressure off you while still ensuring that everything is running smoothly as members start to multiply.

Two-Way Communication Is Key

As you grow your network, you will want to prepare yourself for what many in the industry call "detractors" to healthy community growth. These are the complainers, the fighters, those who seem to dislike everything about the community; yet they stay, complaining loudly.

It is important to remember that the less responsive you are to member queries, the louder the detractors will be. Many are easily dealt with because they are members with legitimate problems they want to see resolved. Success in dealing with these members depends completely on how you respond. We highly recommend you get into the conversation (or "rant") early—as in right away. If you do, you will likely see the tone of your disgruntled member change instantly. Think how you have felt when you had a customer service issue with a company. If an understanding, empathetic representative handles your call or query immediately, it takes the steam out of your displeasure in a single call. But think how you feel when you are kept on hold for ages, have to call back several times, or maybe don't even get a response to your call. Well, now you are the business, and your members are your customers. Treat them the same way you want to be treated.

> ### Words of Wisdom
>
> *It's not all sunshine and roses.*
> *Interacting can be time-consuming.*
>
> —GINA BIANCHINI, CEO, NING

CLICK TIP

Remember the rule: When customers are happy with your service, they tell about two people. When they are unhappy with your service, they tell 11 people . . . or more.

Again, if you are not able to keep up with the members' needs and requests, it would be a good idea to consider recruiting a community manager or moderator.

When to Report or Ban

At the other end of the detractors you have the "trolls." These sorry souls seem to lurk on most popular sites, coming out from their rocks now and again to spew some (completely nonproductive) venom at you, a member, or the community in general. Bloggers have been dealing with them for years, so as a person launching a networking business, you can benefit from their pain: most networking platforms provide the means to permanently ban a troll from your site. *Do not choose a platform or software package that does not have this feature.*

As the creator of your community, it is up to you to develop a policy code from the beginning about what is—and is not—acceptable behavior at your pad. You set the tone.

The most effective way to monitor and control negative behavior on your site is to use a system of reporting (by members) and banning (by you or other site administrators). You also need to give your members the ability to monitor and delete, if necessary, what other members or visitors post on their own profile, photos, videos, and blogs. One of the reasons we recommend Ning is that this feature is automatically built into every network created on its platform. Members on a Ning-run network have the option to report an issue on every page. The online form, shown in Figure 11.1, is very easy to use. The network creator or designated administrator(s) gets e-mailed automatically all of

CLICK TIP

According to Kaiser Wahab, a partner at Wahab & Medenica LLC and a legal expert and lecturer on social networking: "[Online networking sites] should be wary of their complaint response time. As part of a settlement with law enforcement officials, Facebook must respond within 24 hours with a detailed response to complainant."

Figure 11.1: **NING ISSUE-REPORTING FORM**

Ning Network Creators

MAIN · INVITE · MY PAGE · MEMBERS · FORUM · GROUPS · NOT

Report an Issue

Use this form to report an issue to Ning, the creator of Ning Network Creators.

Report an Issue

Type of Issue ⊙ Adult ⊙ Abusive ⊙ Bug ⊙ Fraud ⊙ Spam ⊙ Other

Describe Your Issue

[Send Report]

the members' reports. They can also delete any inappropriate content or complete member profile at any time.

Any community is going to have a small but vocal minority that will attempt to hijack your concept and take you and your community in a way neither you (nor the majority of your members) actually want to go.

We have seen more than a few network communities go by the wayside because the owner or creator reacted too quickly to what seemed like a large "campaign" for a certain feature or service. What they didn't do was determine the actual percentage of people who wanted the change(s). Sometimes that number was a lot smaller than it sounded, and the network found out—way too late—that it had alienated and infuriated more than 90 percent of their membership.

The detractors will not succeed if you have 1) a clear vision in your mind of what your community is all about (see Chapter 3) and 2) a system in place to be able to determine what the overall membership of your site wants from its community.

Benchmarking

Speaking about the early stages of his successful online networking businesses, Ted Rheingold, founder of Dogster.com and Catster.com, says:

At first I thought Dogster would be a passive business. If I just got the website up and running, people would use it to upload their pet photos, I would find advertisers and deposit the checks. But people wanted more features, or some members created problems for other members—such as giving them unsolicited advice about what they should or shouldn't do with their pets. I never wanted the experience to be offensive to anyone. I spent a lot of time in the beginning telling people what not to do.

Now we have a codified set of Participation Guidelines, and if someone breaks one we let them know that they broke it. We have put some members into a "time out", and if they want to come back to the community, they have to agree that they will always abide by the guidelines. They usually do.

The first feature set we created was just posting and sharing. There really wasn't much communication or community. I had big plans all laid out of what was going to happen in versions 2, 3, 4, and 5 . . . then I started getting e-mail from the members about what they wanted. And it wasn't what I thought. My road map went out the window; the members became my guide. If it seemed like more than 50 percent wanted a certain feature (not just a vocal minority, I made that mistake in the beginning), that's what I worked on. For the first couple of years almost every feature launched was at the demand of the community. It was completely user-driven.

As it evolved, we would take all the members' common ideas, as well as ideas we saw working in other communities, and we would send out a survey to 1,000 members: "Here are ten features we are thinking of implementing, but we can only do three at this time. What three features are the most important to you?"

When we started Dogster, people also started putting up photos of their cats. It was the community that made the rule it should only be dogs on Dogster. So that was one of the first changes I made in my road map: I decided to create Catster.

Some people don't necessarily want to make a blog on their dog (or cat). SO we have features now for people outside our core customer base. A lot of people come to our sites to learn more about a health problem their pet is having.

One of the things we are also doing is making the site more appropriate for advertisers to work with, because we have become large enough to be able to build longer and more large-scale business relationships with our partners.

But we never forget who our core members are, and we don't go too long without adding or improving features they like and request.

I highly recommend that if something starts working and the customers want it, do it! Don't just do what some MBA consultant says. Your members will let you know what they want and what will keep them coming back to your site.

Customer service in your online networking business is really not that complicated. Just remember to offer something of clear value from the beginning. Make the sign-up process easy and clear—and make it very easy for people to connect with each other right away. Make sure your site launches with quality content that is related to the theme of your network. Welcome feedback from your members; in fact, hungrily request it!

Finally, make sure that you remember to reward your members for their continued enthusiastic presence.

Chapter 12

Face-to-Face and Online Networks

*M*any face-to-face networking businesses have developed their own online components well after their inception . . . and many online networks have naturally evolved to regional groups that meet in person on a regular or sporadic basis.

Most of the country's top networking experts agree that an online network can grow faster and have longer life if the network offers its members face-to-face meeting opportunities, making the networking more "real" at a fundamental level.

> ## Words of Wisdom
>
> *Networks that merge online and face-to-face networking are the wave of the future, and have the greatest chance of success in the long term.*
>
> —Dr. Ivan Misner, Founder, BNI

And those networks that have traditionally only met in person can extend relationships by adding an online component.

In the June 1, 2008, edition of the Sunday *New York Times*, two different sections featured articles about networking groups: One was Drinking Liberally, a group touting "liberal politics and pints" that meets every Thursday night in Manhattan. It celebrated its fifth anniversary in late May 2008. Thanks to social networking, the group has grown from two guys meeting over a pitcher of beer to discuss politics to a national organization: there more than 251 chapters spread all over the United States (and at least one in every state, as well as Washington DC, according to the group's website: drinkingliber ally.org). The founders sell logo products in their own online store and have just introduced the "Liberal Card" that provides discounts and special offers to card-carriers by various sponsors and vendors.

The second group, Nerd Night, is smaller. It meets monthly at a pub in NYC's East Village. The organizer books speakers to lecture on things scientific, technological . . . in essence, "nerdy" topics. The event is becoming more popular every month (and a mention in the *Times* certainly will draw a few more visitors). But, imagine if the founder decided to add online networking component to promote the concept, and perhaps encourage nerds all over the country to unite by creating similar events elsewhere.

A "Walled Garden" Network Community

BNI (bni.com), the world's largest business networking organization, was founded in 1985 by Ivan Misner on the premise of "Givers Gain"—if I refer business to you, you are more likely to want to refer business to me. Members meet weekly to share contacts, ideas, and support, and to pass referrals to each other. As there is only one member per profession allowed in a given chapter, there are many different chapters, meeting on either Tuesday, Wednesday, or Thursday (mostly) mornings.

Since its inception, the group has grown from a single meeting in 1985 of about four professionals (including Dr. Misner) in Southern California to more than 105,000 members in 5,000 chapters around the world (in May 2008, Kenya and South Korea brought the total number of countries with BNI chapters to 39). In New York City alone, there are nearly 50 chapters.

Misner embraced online networking very early in BNI's inception, encouraging members to be part of Yahoo! Groups, Ecademy.com, and LinkedIn, among other groups, and he keeps BNI involved in the latest online networking trends. Because BNI is a franchise, many chapters have formed their own online presences, with places for members to make their own pages and connect with other members online, as an enhancement of their face-to-face meetings.

BNI is now forging even further into online networking. Launching fully in mid-2009 (but in beta-test phase right now) is BNIConnect (bniconnect.com), the organization's largest online project to date. Using the tagline *Local Business— Global Network™*, Misner calls the project a "walled garden social network for business." The site will offer all of BNI's blogs, podcasts, newsletters, and member updates in one place, as well as a chance for members who would normally just promote their businesses to their own chapters to promote, instead, to members all over the world. The network is a walled garden because members will only be able to participate in BNIConnect if they are active members of a local BNI chapter. If they discontinue their BNI membership, they will no longer have access to BNIConnect.

With the advent of these networks, "small businesses can really market on a global level now," says Misner.

In his book *Truth or Delusion*, he cites a 2006 study that showed the average ages of people in networking groups who owned their own businesses. The study showed a perfect bell curve, with the median age being 45 years old. As you can see in the graphic in Figure 12.1, 37 percent of business owners are in the 20 to 39 age range. This is the generation to watch, particularly if you are considering starting an online networking group catering to business professionals in your area.

> **CLICK TIP**
>
> Connect with a network that already exists, and leverage existing networks online to feed and build a sustainable community.

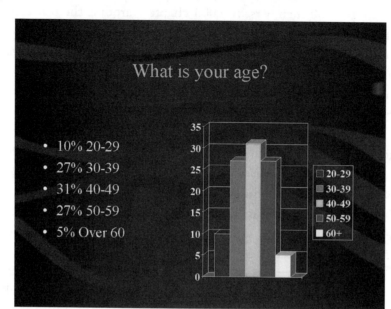

Figure 12.1: **AVERAGE AGE OF BUSINESS OWNERS**

What is your age?

- 10% 20-29
- 27% 30-39
- 31% 40-49
- 27% 50-59
- 5% Over 60

Source: *Truth or Delusion,* Ivan Misner (Nelson Business Press, 2006)

The oldest members of the Baby Boomer generation (born approximately 1946–64) are now at retirement age, and the Generation X (born approximately 1964–81) are entering the mid-points of their careers. While both of these groups have had heavy exposure to computers and the internet, it cannot be compared to that of Generation Y (born approximately 1981–2001, also known as "Millennials" or the "Internet Generation"), who have virtually no knowledge of a time without computers and the internet. Leading his face-to-face networking business into the next century, Misner has looked at these demographics and firmly believes that the newest wave of business networkers will demand an online component to their daily networking.

On the flip side, building a face-to-face component into your networking business will help solidify relationships, and give members a further reason to grow and develop within your network. Why choose your network when there are so many others out there? Myra Norton, CEO of Community Analytics, a research organization that focuses on mapping influence networks among all kinds of audiences, feels that online networks have become what websites used to be: A "dime a dozen":

> *Why would I choose a particular site versus the countless others out there? What will be the value I receive? In the marketplace, content does provide a big piece, but it is also—and perhaps even more—about the relationships I am able to build and nurture there. I need to have some trusted relationship that says this is a valuable network to participate in. Yes, you can form some connections and trust through a person you have met purely online, but it is definitely not the same as meeting someone in person.*

A successful merger of online/offline networking depends also on the nature of the network. If you build a network for entrepreneurs, Norton says, having an offline component is the best way to keep the venture relevant and valuable to members. You might only set up an annual meeting or perhaps have four smaller, regional get-togethers if you form a national online network as opposed to a regional one. The bottom line is getting your members to connect and stay connected, and the best way to do that is by capitalizing on relationships that already exist and really mean something to people.

The first thing you need to do is make it easy for your participants: set up opportunities for them to meet. You can even make this a revenue source for yourself, if you plan "meetings" for the members of your networking group by setting up the venue and travel arrangements. Acting as "group leader" is another great revenue source.

Let's go back to that hypothetical network created for lovers of Burgundy wines we discussed in Chapter 9. This type of network lends itself perfectly to an online/face-to-face construction. Your members will send in tips on their favorite wines or restaurants (in the United States or the Burgundy region of France) that have the best wine menus. But what if you created your network so that groups could form in different geographical regions, meeting weekly or monthly to have dinner and wine at different restaurants, or set up wine tasting events at different venues? You could charge a fee for these events, all payable through the website, and watch the network grow from this very dynamic merger of online and face-to face components.

Take it a step further and set up gatherings for your Burgundy wine connoisseurs all over the country, complete with travel/hotel/restaurant packages. And once a year, you could offer the *pièce de resistance*: A conference at a winery/estate in—you guessed it—France's beautiful Burgundy! Imagine if you made it easy for your members to set up all hotels, airfare, restaurants, etc. through your site? You would be able to make a commission on every transaction.

Build "Street Cred" for Your Online Community with Face-to-Face Networking

MNG (My Networking Group, networkingmng.com) is a rapidly growing networking group in New York City that is strongly embracing the concept of online networking to complement its bi-weekly meetings. Founded in May 2007 by Ross Karp and Robert Remin, it has rapidly outgrown its venue and is now in the process of splitting into different sections, including ones for B2B (business to business) and B2C (business to consumer), as well as sections for members representing businesses that are more vertical or industry-focused, such as healthcare. The group's leaders feel that having this flexibility will allow for the most focus and greatest long-term chances for success.

MNG uses the term "section" in lieu of "chapter" to accentuate the point that, while a member may belong to one section, all members are considered part of the group as a whole, as an aggregate of the MNG membership. As the group continues to grow, it is in the process of implementing its online networking component. The initial website will evolve to include advanced features, such as message boards, blogs, listings for "open opportunities," and data-mining capabilities. Members will have their own pages and be able to designate public and private file areas, allowing them to choose what members and nonmembers will be able to see. Initially, access to the site will be a premium for paying members and the group's leadership does not rule out the addition of banner ads as the membership expands beyond New York City and site traffic continues to grow.

According to one of the group's leaders, Ron Rudin of DDR Enterprises, MNG's philosophy is as follows: The more people you network with, the wider your reach. He strongly advocates a combination of face-to-face and online networking: "Having a networking organization that is solely either one or the other is like having a PBJ sandwich with only the peanut butter or only the jelly—you need both components for a completely enjoyable experience."

So what does this concept mean for you? How can you build a business under this concept? You could take an existing interest or professional group and develop an online network around it. It could be as simple as building a site for the group of moms who meet with their kids for play dates: Imagine putting together a website where people in your area could not only find play dates, but also trade babysitting, ask/offer advice, or just connect to alleviate the isolation many stay-at-home moms may feel?

You could organize an evening event "for moms only" at a local venue, and charge a flat fee for attendance, which could pay for the expenses and even a small stipend for yourself. As the meetings grow, the more money you can make.

Meetup (meetup.com) was founded in 2002 by Scott Heiferman, Mat Meeker, and Peter Kamali. Simply put, Meetup is a website that allows users—for free—to search meetings in their area on topics that interest them. The bigger the geographic area, the more available meetings. If members do not see a particular meeting they want in their area, no problem . . . they can organize one themselves! For that service, the organizer pays $19 a month. Meetup is continually expanding its services to allow organizers to charge what they want for the meetings, and many organizers have grown their groups to a point where they actually make a living managing them! And here's the best part: Many of the groups that developed through Meetup have grown nationally through the use of their own online networks.

> ### Words of Wisdom
>
> *A network is tribal. People want to know who their chief is. Facebook started at Harvard because [founder] Mark Zukerberg was at Harvard. A successful online network is a manifestation and construction of a network that already exists outside . . . it has to have "street cred."*
>
> —ELLIOTT MASIE, CEO, MASIE CENTER AND LEARNING CONSORTIUM

> ## Words of Wisdom
>
> *It's really best if you have real face time with your target audience. Speak to them, tell them about your online community plans.*
>
> —Peter Bihr, author of TheWavingCat.com

An offline network can be an excellent "feed" for a new online network. As mentioned previously, the key to the longevity of a network is getting the right members or participants on board in the first place. You may be able to build your network amazingly quickly if you offer a new online component to an already-existing network.

As you venture for the first time into the exciting world of new media and online networks, if you create a network that is accompanied by local or regional meetings, it will be at the most fundamental level more *real* to your members. This sense of both place *and* purpose will encourage them to stay and bring others into the group, and that contributes to your growth.

Chapter 13

Launching an Online Network for Your Existing Business

*A*s a person with strong entrepreneurial spirit, you may already be running one or more businesses. You may be a solo-preneur, running each by yourself, or you may have employees of varying numbers. Starting an online network within your existing businesses can be a great way to increase the profits of those businesses.

Words of Wisdom

We have done ONAs (Organizational Network Analysis) for groups as small as seven people, and they found the results to be very valuable because what you learn from such a study is not only how those seven individuals are interacting with each other, but how they are each leveraging their personal networks for the good of the groups/company as a whole.

Organizational Network Analysis looks not only at the internal dynamics, but also the impact that each person's personal network (both inside and outside of the company) brings to bear on the success of the organization.

—Myra Norton, CEO, Community Analytics, Inc.

A great number of larger corporations have already discovered that opening up the gateways of communication through an internal social network has allowed them to learn more about employees, particularly their hidden talents, talents that may be tapped into as the company grows.

An increasing number of small (1–500 employee) businesses are embracing online networks, particularly as the workforce becomes more and more filled with employees who have spent their entire lives online.

If you own a small business, or businesses, one of the main reasons you should consider adding an online networking component is that the best time to make an online network part of your company culture is when the company is small. It can then stay in place and grow along with your company. As a small business owner, you probably wear multiple hats and, even with your handy PDA, you may have a difficult time gathering all the information you need about your employees in a single place. By utilizing an online network you can keep track of—and have immediate access to—information about what each employee is currently working on, and what experience they have from previous positions.

Your company may have employees operating from remote locations. This is becoming increasingly common in small businesses. Setting up an internal online network will enable those employees to interact with each other—and with you—without leaving their desks, allowing for more personalization and less isolation.

Finally, as a CEO or owner of more than one small business, implementing an online network gives you the power to gather information across your businesses, search for the best employees for particular tasks, and establish greater collaboration between you and your employees.

Larger businesses are already jumping on the bandwagon, particularly in the last couple of years, but the time is right—and the software is here—for smaller businesses to profit from an internal online networking component as well.

These internal company online networks are dynamic and allow employees to use virtually all the features they would find on Facebook or even LinkedIn, including social networking, tagging, and profile.

While there are many hosted applications that cater to this market segment, one of the most robust services we have found for small businesses is SuccessFactors' Employee Profile. Considered one of the fastest growing public software companies, SuccessFactors (successfactors.com) is a "leading provider of on-demand employee performance and talent management solutions that enable organizations of every size, across every industry and geography, to realize their employees' potential and thus drive business results."

In July 2008, SuccessFactors introduced its Enhanced Talent Management Solution for Small and Mid-Sized Businesses, called Professional Edition ULTRA, that uses:

Web 2.0 technology from some of today's popular and viral consumer-facing applications and social networking sites to make the applications more engaging and fun to use, giving employees the ability to interact with each other similar to social media and networking-type communities.

Figure 13.1 shows an example of an Employee Directory in the Employee Profile product. Note the tags that have been added by the employee (and in some cases, by the employer, particularly in terms of job title or department).

Figure 13.2 shows a view of a sample employee's individual profile. Notice on the right the links to the employee's personal Facebook and LinkedIn profiles. There are other tabs in this view, some of which are completed by the employee, some by the employer.

Finally, Figure 13.3 shows a view of an internal "tag cloud" (see Chapter 9). This cloud is a composite "picture" of all the tags put in by the employees and the employer. Notice in this sample company, there are a lot of people

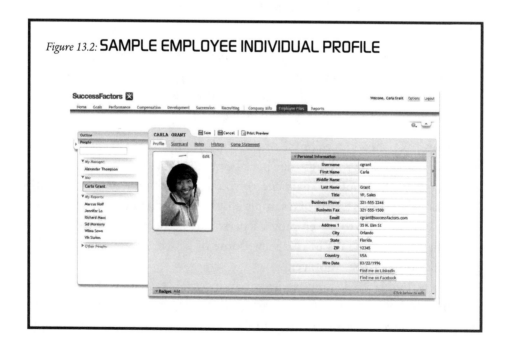

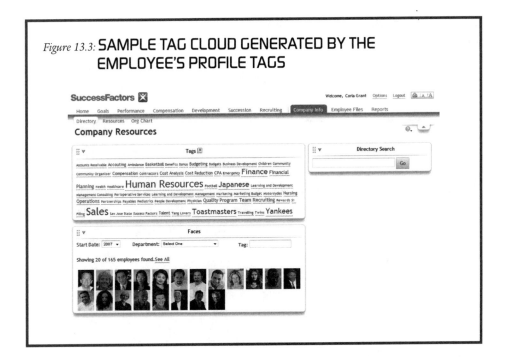

Figure 13.3: **SAMPLE TAG CLOUD GENERATED BY THE EMPLOYEE'S PROFILE TAGS**

involved in the Toastmasters and Yankees fans. A surprising number of people either speak or are interested in Japanese, or have it in their heritage. This is great information if you have the opportunity to do business with or in Japan; and it might not have shown up on the employees' resumes.

The reason we have chosen to highlight SuccessFactors Employee Profile in particular is because of its August 2008 integration with five Google products. These allow companies of all sizes to benefit from cloud computing—there is no software to download, install, or maintain. This has huge

CLICK TIP

As an entrepreneur, you want to be on the lookout for the newest trends that help keep you lean and profitable. Our tip is to keep an eye on the trends of implementing an online network as an integral part of your business and to focus on the increasing number of cloud computing options available to you.

implications for the way small businesses do business. With such integration, employees will not have to switch applications, or even browser tabs, to find information and collaborate with you or with other employees in the business. See the box below for a listing of all the available Google applications.

GOOGLE INTEGRATIONS WITH SUCCESSFACTORS

SuccessFactors designed, developed, and integrated the following five solutions with Google products. The first three are with GoogleApps™ and the other two are integrations with other Google products. The integrations include:

- SuccessFactors and Google Talk™
  To instantly communicate with a manager, members of a team, or others to discuss specific goals, performance reviews, and development/project plans.

- SuccessFactors and Google Calendar™
  To keep track of key events, deadlines against a goal plan, or key dates in the performance review process.

- SuccessFactors and Google Docs™
  For sharing knowledge and promoting collaboration by posting relevant, recommended documents, spreadsheets, and presentations from the SuccessFactors system, making them available to the internal and external audiences through Google Docs™.

- SuccessFactors and Google Book Search™
  Gives employees the tools to control their career development by providing clear visibility into the competencies they need to work on to prepare for future roles, along with relevant, suggested reading through Google Book Search.

- SuccessFactors and Google Maps™
  Helps understand where individuals and teams are located, and to coordinate activities and make informed decisions on deploying talent.

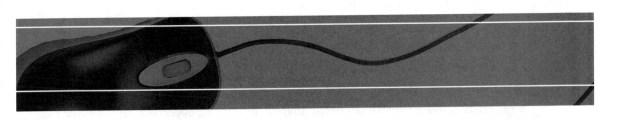

Afterword

*W*e hope you are realizing just how exciting the social and online networking world has become, and how easy it is to put yourself right in the middle of it—whether for business or for pleasure. This book was written with the intent of introducing you to the possibilities that exist in the world of online networks beyond Facebook, MySpace, or the other mega-sites. A single person sitting at a desk in a living room or home office has just as much chance as anyone to profit in this industry.

For the solo-preneur or small business owner, however, the keys are to identify a niche area of interest and to realize that the way to succeed in growing a successful online network is to focus first and foremost on the *community*. There are a lot of sites competing for attention; some are empty and un-updated, while others are vibrant with lots of action and dynamic interaction between the members. Which ones do you think can command serious ad dollars or even investor capital?

Picture a town that has not been kept up: Signs or streetlights are broken, storefronts are boarded up, and there's not a single fun place to gather to meet and interact with people. Pretty quickly, people will begin to move away to other towns that offer a warm, welcoming, and lively place. Those are the kinds of towns where they will gravitate, maybe even "move in," put down roots—and invite family and friends to join them!

Remember to build your community with a "Town Square" approach. Start with a central gathering place (your homepage) that will attract visitors . . . and make them want to hang around for a bit to see what all the buzz is about. Just as a thriving town offers great parks, housing, and utilities that work all the time in all kinds of conditions, so must your network have exciting features that help members interact with each other and a sound technological platform that ensures there will be little or no downtime due to technical glitches.

If you've been anywhere near a computer or the internet in the past few years, you cannot help but notice how fast things are changing in the "cybersphere." As you begin to build and grow your online community, there are many online resources included throughout the book and in the Resources section where you will find a vast amount of information.

■ ■ ■

I have always been an early adopter of the newest gems the evolving internet has to offer. However, my life changed dramatically as I have become more and more involved in the social media and online networking industry. It is so exciting to be involved in the newest way human beings communicate! Feel free to contact me anytime to share your stories!

—Julien Sharp
stylocreative.com
julien@stylocreative.com

Find me on Twitter: twitter.com/juliensharp
Or Facebook: profile.to/juliensharp/
Or LinkedIn: linkedin.com/in/juliensharp

SECTION IV

Appendices

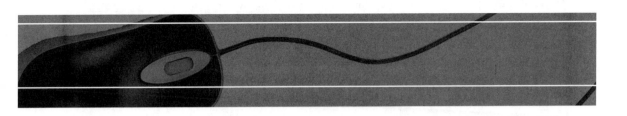

Resources

Must-Visit Websites

blog.dogster.com: Dogster's corporate blog.

blog.ning.com: Ning's corporate blog.

doshdosh.com: Offers internet marketing and blogging tips, as well as social media strategies.

mashable.com: Mashable! The Social Networking Blog.

problogger.net: Blog tips and news for the professional and hobby blogger.

readwriteweb.com: Web apps, web technology trends, social networking.

searchengineland.com: Hub for news and information about search engine marketing, optimization, and how search engines work for searchers.

socialmediaheadhunter.com: Great site if you want to hire staff for your online networking business.

socialmediatoday.com: The web's best thinkers on social media and Web 2.0.

socialmediatodayllc.com: Social media in the B2B world.

strategicast.com: Strategic thoughts on social media marketing.

techcrunch.com: Dedicated to obsessively profiling and reviewing internet products and companies.

thewavingcat.com: Social Media, Web 2.0, and Digital Life.

webware.com: Cool Web apps for everyone. CNET's blog about Web 2.0.

web-strategist.com/blog: How web tools enable companies to connect with customers.

Two Must-Read Links to Two Articles in Two Must-Read Magazines

"Ning's Infinite Ambition" by Adam L. Penenberg, *Fast Company*, May 2008; fastcompany.com/magazine/125/nings-infinite-ambition.html.

"The Long Tail" by Chris Anderson, *Wired*, October 2004; wired.com/wired /archive/12.10/tail.html

Must-See Advertising and Marketing Sites

blogher.com

federatedmedia.net

socialmedia.com

Must-Consider-Attending
Industry Conferences

Blog World Expo: blogworldexpo.com

BlogHer Conference: blogher.com/blogher_conference/conf

International Conference on Weblogs and Social Media: icwsm.org

Internet Week New York: internetweekny.com

Search Marketing Expo: searchmarketingexpo.com/social

Social Media Conference: socialmediaconference.com

SXSW Interactive Conference: sxsw.com/interactive

Must-Have Books for
Your Reference Library

Allen, Scott, Jay T. Deragon, Margaret G. Orem, and Carter F. Smith. *The Emergence of the Relationship Economy: The New Order of Things to Come* (Happy About.info, 2008).

Anderson, Chris. *The Long Tail: Why the Future of Business Is Selling Less of More* (New York: Hyperion, 2008).

Canton, James. *The Extreme Future: The Op Trends That Will Shape the World in the Next 20 Years* (New York: Plume, 2007).

Godin, Seth. *Meatball Sundae: Is Your Marketing Out of Sync?* (New York: Portfolio Hardcover, 2007).

Meerman, David, and Scott Welch. *The New Rules of Marketing and PR* (New York: Wiley, 2008).

Misner, Ivan R., Mike Macedonio, and Mike Garrison. *Truth or Delusion* (Nashville, TN: Nelson Business, 2006).

Saffir, Leonard. *PR on a Budget: Free, Cheap, and Worth the Money Strategies for Getting Noticed* (Chicago: Kaplan Business, 2006).

Silver, David. *Smart Start-Ups: How Entrepreneurs and Corporations Can Profit by Starting Online Communities* (New York: Wiley, 2007).

Tapscott, Don, and Anthony D. Williams. *Wikinomics: How Mass Collaboration Changes Everything* (New York: Portfolio, 2007).

Teten, David, and Scott Allen. *The Virtual Handshake: Opening Doors and Closing Deals Online* (New York: Amacom, 2005).

Winke, Jeff. *PR Idea Book: 50 Proven Tools That Really Work* (Parker, CO: Outskirts Press, 2006).

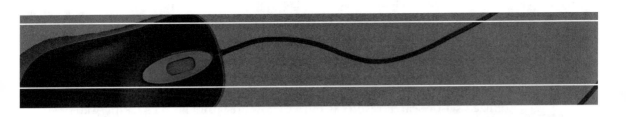

Glossary of Terms

$\mathcal{T}$he following is a comprehensive list of terms that you will want to know as you set off into the world of online networking. Most of the terms have been discussed in the book, but we've also included a few of the more technical terms that, while you may not need to know them to launch your business, you will be glad to know as your business expands and you delve deeper into the technological aspects of what goes into an online network.

Aggregator. A software program or online service that uses a web feed to retrieve syndicated electronic content such as *weblogs, podcasts, vlogs,* and mainstream mass media websites. In the case of a search aggregator, a customized set of search results is retrieved. Aggregators keep checking websites to see if they have been updated; updates are displayed with a title and link to the complete content of the new information.

AJAX (Asynchronous JavaScript and XML). A technique for creating interactive web applications to make web pages feel more responsive. By exchanging small amounts of data with the server there is no need to reload the entire web page each time the user requests a change. This is intended to increase the page's interactivity, speed, and usability.

API (Application Programming Interface). The interface by which an application accesses operating systems and other services. An API is defined at source code level. It can also provide an interface between a high-level language and lower-level utilities and services, for instance, by translating parameter lists from one format to another (one computer language to another).

Atom. A standard protocol for disseminating information via blogs. The Atom Syndication Format is an XML language used for web feeds (see *Aggregator*), while the Atom Publishing Protocol (AtomPub or APP) is an HTTP-based protocol for creating and updating web resources.

Avatar. A computer user's representation of him or herself, whether in the form of a three-dimensional model for gaming; a two-dimensional icon or picture, which may be a graphic animation or rendering—used on internet forums or other communities; or a text construct found on early systems such as MUDs. It is an "object" representing the embodiment of the user. It can also refer to the personality connected with the screen name, or handle, of an internet user. Abbreviations include "av" and "avi."

Banner ad. An advertisement graphically splashed across the full width of the top or bottom of a web page.

Blog. A contraction of web log. A journal posted on the web, usually arranged in reverse chronological order. More generally, a tool that makes web publishing easy.

Blogger. Someone who writes a *blog*.

Blogging. The activity of updating and composing a *blog*.

Blogosphere. The internet community of all *bloggers* and *blogs*.

Blogroll. The section of a *blog* that lists the sites that the *blogger* reads regularly. Doc Searls coined the term as a reference to "logrolling," defined as the exchange of favors or praise.

CAN-SPAM Act of 2003. U.S. antispam legislation that stands for Controlling the Assault of Non-Solicited Pornography and Marketing.

CDA. Communications Decency Act, providing protection against defamation claims.

Character. In the context of this book, integrity, clarity of motives, consistency of behavior, openness, discretion, and trustworthiness of an internet user.

Chat. Real-time text communication, much like instant messaging, except that it usually indicates multiple participants meeting at a common virtual "place," such as a *web forum* or chat room. Each participant's comments are repeated immediately and simultaneously on the screens of all other participants in the same chat room.

Clicks. The measurable quantity in online marketing that demonstrates how many times users click their cursors on a seller's ad or the link to a seller's website. See *Pay-per-click advertising*.

Clique. A small group of people tied to one another by common characteristics, usually within a larger group.

Closed network. See *Closure*.

Closure. A network with closure is one in which everyone is connected so that no one member can escape the notice of the other members; also one in which people share the same beliefs, geography, or industry.

Cloud computing. Online software that need no software to download, install, or maintain (also known as software-as-a-service).

Contact management software. Software that helps individuals aggregate and analyze data about people with whom one is associated: not only name, phone, and e-mail, but also notes on personality, sales progress, and other factors.

COPPA. Children's Online Privacy Protection Act.

CPC (Cost per click). The amount you are paid per user *click* of an ad on your site. This amount corresponds to the advertiser's bid rate for winning the right to place that ad on your site and will vary.

CPM (Cost per thousand). A flat rate paid by an advertiser per thousand ad impressions that appear on your site. This fee is usually paid monthly.

Crawler. A virtual robot (run by an intricate online software program) that searches the web for new and updated web pages. As the crawler finds pages, it places them in a central database, usually for the benefit of a search engine.

Cross-linking. Communicates content that a site owner considers important. Linking between two sites can increase visibility in search engines.

Cross-posting. The act of posting the same message to more than one group or list, sometimes within the same website but under different headings or forum titles.

Degree. In social network analysis, the number of steps between one individual and another. Knowing someone directly is a first-degree relationship. Connecting to the first-degree relations of your first-degree relations creates a second-degree relationship, and so on. See *Online social network*.

DMCA. Digital Millennium Copyright Act, providing protections against copyright infringement claims.

Emoticons. A combination of text characters meant to represent a facial expression. People use emoticons in e-mails, etc. to convey meaning. Some examples: :-) = smile, ;-) = wink, ;-/ = wry smile, !-) = imaginative.

Enterprise whuffie. The reputation that employees can acquire by becoming known as experts in a given area. The term was possibly invented by Steve Gillmor, a technology journalist.

Flame. A deliberately hostile and insulting online message, as displayed on blogs, forums, social networking sites, and other virtual spheres.

FOAF (Friend of a Friend). A data file format that stores personal profile information and relationships. Software developers use it to make such information portable between various systems.

Folksonomy. A system used to categorize and retrieve web pages, photographs, web links, and other virtual content using open-ended labels called *tags*. The process of folksonomic tagging is intended to make a body of information increasingly easily to search, discover, and navigate over time. A well-developed folksonomy is ideally accessible as a shared vocabulary that is both originated by and familiar to primary users. Two widely cited examples of websites using folksonomic tagging are Flickr and del.icio.us.

Google Bot. A *search bot* (*web crawler*) used specifically by Google.

HTML. The code in which web pages are written.

IM. See *Instant messaging.*

Information. The data that you have about the people you know.

Instant messaging. Real-time virtual, textual communication, generally person-to-person. Often abbreviated as IM, which may denote instant messaging or, sometimes, AOL's instant messaging platform, AOL IM.

ISP (Internet Service Provider). A company that provides internet access to people or corporations.

Link.
1. In the context of social networks, the relationship between two nodes for the network.
2. In the context of the web, a piece of text that connects to another document (or section of the current document) or launches an action

(such as executing a predefined search, sending an e-mail, or moving to another web page or site).

List server. A program that accepts an e-mail from a user and forwards it to all members of the list server's mailing list. The list server typically also generates an archive.

Long tail trend (in a social networking context). This term was coined by Chris Anderson, editor-in-chief of *Wired* magazine, who said "there's money to be made in the long tail of niche offerings." There is very high demand for a very small number of "blockbusters" but, though the demand for "niche offerings" is much less, it is also much longer (the "tail" of the curve as shown in a chart depicting demand), meaning that a lot of smaller business offerings can still make money in their specific niches.

Mash-up. A new breed of web-based applications designed to mix at least two different services from disparate and even competing websites, combining multiple sources of data into a single tool. For example, a mash-up could take traffic data from one source on the internet and overlay it on maps from Yahoo!, Microsoft, Google, or any content provider.

The architecture of mash-up web applications is always composed of three parts:

1. *The content provider.* The source of the data; data is made available using an API and different web formats such as RSS and REST
2. *The mash-up site.* The web application; the mash-up provides the new service using different data sources that are not owned by it.
3. *The client web browser.* The user interface of the mashup; in a web application, the content can be mashed by the client web browsers using client-side web language, for example, JavaScript.

Metcalfe's law. The principle that the value of a communications system grows approximately as the square of the number of its users (N^2).

Moore's law. A concept introduced by Intel co-founder Gordon E. Moore in a 1965 paper: The number of transistors on a chip, or the amount of data etc. a computer chip can hold, will double about every two years. At the same time, the price of chips will decrease.

Multiplex. An adjective indicating that there is more one type of relationship between two nodes.

Netiquette. Etiquette of interacting with others virtually.

Network. In the context of human relationships and this book, a network is the set of relationships that individuals need to get tasks done, to advance in an organization, or to grow as people.

Network Valuation Formula[SM] Formula developed by David Teten to analyze and value a social network.

Networking. Developing relationships for the purpose of supporting one another in achieving group and personal goals. Networking has also been widely adopted by the network marketing industry to refer specifically to the practice of network marketing.

Networking groups. Organized groups in which people to get to know one another for business purposes.

News aggregator. See *News reader.*

News reader. A website or software tool used to combine data feeds from multiple blogs or websites into a single feed, which may be downloaded or aggregated in one place online.

Node. In a network, any point (e.g., a person) where two lines meet. If one individual knows two others, that individual is a node between the two.

Number. How many people to whom one is directly linked in a network, i.e., the combined number of *strong* and *weak ties.*

One-click buying. The technique of allowing customers to make online purchases with a single click of the mouse because the payment information needed to complete the purchase has been previously entered by the user. More particularly, it allows an online shopper using an internet marketplace to purchase an item without having to use shopping-cart software. Instead of manually inputting billing and shipping information for a purchase, a user can use one-click buying to use a predefined address and credit card number to purchase one or more items. The concept was pioneered by Amazon.

Online community. See *Virtual community.*

Online social network. Any network of people that is entirely virtual (e.g., an online community that does not hold regular, in-person meetings) or partially virtual (e.g., the community may hold regular, in-person meetings). People can build their personal networks online using any of the technologies we discuss in this book. For example, a group of bloggers discussing a common point constitutes an online social network.

Open-source software. Any computer software whose source code is available under a license (or arrangement, such as the public domain) so that any user may study, change, or improve the software, or redistribute it in modified or unmodified form. It is often developed in a public, collaborative manner.

Pay-per-click advertising. Advertising model used on search engines, advertising networks, and content websites and blogs, where advertisers only pay when a user actually clicks on an ad to visit the advertiser's website.

Permalink. A permanent link on a blog that will link to a given post after that post is moved off the front page and into archives. Some blogs use the word "permalink," but it is also common to use the time of the post or the "#" symbol.

PHP (Hypertext Preprocessor). Computer scripting language originally designed for producing dynamic web pages.

Platform. Software that makes services available to other software programs through *Application Programming Interfaces* (APIs). Basically, the software code on which third-party applications function, such as Microsoft Windows or Mac OS.

Podcast. A media file (audio or video) that is distributed over the internet using syndication feeds for playback on portable media players and personal computers. The host or author of a podcast is often called a podcaster. Though podcasters' websites may also offer direct download or streaming of their content, a podcast is distinguished from other digital audio formats by its ability to be downloaded automatically, using software capable of reading feed formats such as *RSS* or *Atom.*

Podcasting's initial appeal was to allow individuals to distribute their own "radio shows," but the system quickly became used in a wide variety of other ways, including distribution of school lessons; official and unofficial audio tours of museums; conference meeting alerts and updates; and by police departments to distribute public safety messages.

RDF. The standard data format for publishing and syndicating headlines and short content. It is usually used for distribution of blog posts.

Reed's law. The principle that the value of large networks, particularly social networks, can scale exponentially with the size of the network (approximately 2N).

Relationship capital management software. Helps individuals track those with whom they interact online, and learn about other people to whom your network can provide access. For instance, if you want to reach a particular target person who is a few degrees away from you, these tools help you determine who can introduce you to that person and provide background information on them. The software typically analyzes relationships by spidering through e-mails, IMs, and other digital records.

Relevance. An acquaintance's value, defined as their ability to contribute to an individual's specific goals, interests, or needs.

RSS. Originally "RDF Site Summary," but also commonly referred to as "Really Simple Syndication." RSS is a standard data format for publishing and syndicating headlines and short content. It is usually used for distribution of blog posts.

RSS reader. A news reader for RSS feeds.

Search bot (web crawler). Program that automatically browses the internet in a methodical manner. Collects a copy of all the visited pages for processing and indexing by search engines to allow for faster searches.

SEO (Search Engine Optimization). The process of optimizing one's website for a search engine, i.e., driving more web traffic to the site through search engines for the purpose of generating more business. SEO companies are a new and booming industry offering services to help improve a site's SEO.

Shared web hosting. Allows many websites to reside on a single server connected to the internet. Each individual site is partitioned, or given its own section, to keep it separate from other sites. This service is more economical than having an individual site on an individual server, because the websites share in the cost of the server maintenance.

Signature file. Text that is automatically added to every online message sent. It usually includes an individual's name, organization, e-mail address, phone number, and frequently a physical address or website.

Site hosting. See *Web hosting service.*

Slashdot effect. The phenomenon of a popular website linking to a smaller site, causing the smaller site to slow down or even temporarily close due to the increased traffic. The name stems from the huge influx of web traffic that results from the technology news site Slashdot linking to underpowered websites. However, it has been used to describe the same effect when generated by other websites or metablogs such as Fark, StumbleUpon, and Digg, leading to terms such as the "Digg effect," or the link becoming "Farked" or "Stumbled." Sites that are maintained on shared hosting services often fail when confronted with the Slashdot effect. Also known as "slashdotting."

Social bookmarks. A web-based service to share internet bookmarks. Social bookmarking sites are a popular way to store, classify, share, and search links through the practice of *folksonomy* techniques. Many social bookmarking services allow users to subscribe to web feeds based on *tags*, or a collection of tag terms, so that subscribers become aware of new resources as they are noted, tagged, and classified by other users.

Social capital. The collective value of all social networks and the inclinations that arise from these networks to do things for each other ("norms of reciprocity").

Social graph. A term coined by Mark Zuckerberg, founder of Facebook: "The network of connections and relationships between people on [Facebook]."

It can be expressed in code or software applications and is used by software developers to improve and create online social networks.

Social media. An umbrella term that defines the various activities that integrate technology, social interaction, and the construction of words, pictures, videos, and audio. This interaction and the manner in which information is presented depend on the varied perspectives and "building" of shared meaning, as people share their stories and understandings. Social media can take many different forms. Examples include: internet forums, message boards, web logs, vlogs, wikis, podcasts, pictures, and video, to name a few. Examples of social media applications are Google Groups, Wikipedia, MySpace, Facebook, Last.fm, YouTube, and Second Life.

Social network. Any group of people acquainted with one another, ranging from casual acquaintances to close family bonds.

Social network analysis. The mapping and measuring of relationships between people, groups, organizations, computers, or other information-processing entities. The nodes in the network are the people and groups, while the links show relationships or flows between the nodes.

Social network site. Virtual communities in which individuals can see more than one degree away. These sites are a subset of virtual communities in general.

Social network software. See *Social software.*

Social networking services. Services (primarily websites) that allow users to see more than one degree away.

Social software. Websites and software tools that allow users to discover, extend, manage, communicate in, or apply leverage to social networks. These include blogs, social networking sites, virtual communities, relationship capital management software, biography analysis software, and many more. Some people use this term for the software used to run online communities and online dating sites, but this use is not appropriate for the purposes of this book.

Software-as-a-service. See *Cloud computing.*

Spam. Unsolicited bulk e-mail (UBE), usually sent to thousands (or millions) of recipients. It is also known as "unsolicited commercial e-mail (UCE)," although some spam is used for political advocacy or chain letters. By definition, spam is sent without the permission of the recipients. In the context of virtual communities, spam refers not only to e-mails, but also to posting advertising in a discussion forum that does not expressly allow advertising.

Spambot. A program used by spammers to automatically collect e-mail addresses from websites and add them to their database. These programs are the reason users are discouraged from placing e-mail addresses on a public website.

Spammers. Internet users who send *spam.*

Spamming. The act of sending or posting spam.

Spider. See *Crawler.*

Spoofing. The falsification of an e-mail header (originating address) so that the e-mail appears to have originated from someone or somewhere other than the real source. Spammers often use this technique so recipients will open spam rather than immediately deleting it.

Strength. The closeness of the relationship between an individual and an acquaintance. This reflects the degree of trust and reciprocity in the relationship.

Strong tie. See *Tie.*

Structural equivalence. Two people are "structurally equivalent" if they each have the same relationships to all other people within their organization. For example, two vice presidents of purchasing for ladies blouses working for Bloomingdales are almost perfectly structurally equivalent. They have the same job title, same function, and interact with similar people almost every day.

Structural hole. The weak connections between clusters of densely connected people. People with these connections can become brokers between the clusters.

Tag. A relevant keyword or term associated with a piece of information (such as a picture, article, website, or video clip), thus describing the item. Typically, an item will have more than one tag associated with it. Tags are chosen informally and personally by the creator or the consumer of the item, not as part of a formally defined classification scheme.

Tag clouds. Word lists that graphically represent the most sought-after or relevant tags on your site or blog. More relevant or searched-for terms are highlighted in a larger font or a different color.

Tie. Family, close friends, and close professional colleagues whom one has, typically, known for a long time and sees regularly, and who frequently reciprocate advice, support, and other informal and formal "gifts."

TrackBack. A system of letting blog owners know that you have quoted, referenced, or used their post for something in your post. This is called "track-backing" or "pinging" their post. This is polite to the original source, expedites discussion, and drives traffic to your blog.

Troll. A person who intentionally posts messages that create controversy or anger, without adding any value to the discussion.

Trolling. The act of being a *troll*.

User Generated Content (UGC). Content produced by the general public, as opposed to being compiled, written, and published by traditional media professionals.

Viral expansion loop. Concept based on the premise that if you set up an online network, you have no choice but to invite people to join it. In turn, those people will invite others to join, and so on.

Virtual community. Group of people that congregates and interacts primarily, or exclusively, virtually.

Virtual reality (VR). Technology that allows a user to interact with a computer-simulated environment, be it real or imagined. The simulated environment can be similar to the real world—for example, simulations for pilot or combat training—or it can differ significantly from reality, as in VR games.

Vlog. Video blogs that primarily feature video shorts instead of text. Users can sign up to receive regular video downloads from vlogs; for instance, the new Apple iTunes podcasting feature supports vlog subscriptions.

Vlogging. The activity of updating a *vlog*.

Weak ties. See *Tie*.

Web 2.0. The second generation of the internet. The internet has improved over time and allows for the invention of more elaborate services, such as blogging, video and audio broadcasts, wikis, and social networking sites. In a Web 2.0 world, there is much more emphasis on user-driven content; i.e., there are more services available that let people collaborate and share information online. Ultimately, Web 2.0 services are expected to replace desktop computing applications for many purposes.

Web 2.0 tools. "Tool" is used here as shorthand for a software application on a computer, and also for applications that are web-based.

Web crawler. A web program that automatically and systematically "crawls" or scans the web in order to index websites and information, usually for use by search engines. Web crawlers gather data such as keywords to aid searching and archiving. Also, bot, web spider, web robot. See also *Search bot*.

Web feed. Allows readers to access a site automatically when looking for new content and then post updates about that new content to another site. This provides a way for users to keep up with the latest and hottest information posted on different sites. Content distributors syndicate a web feed, thereby allowing users to subscribe to it. For most web feeds, RSS, RDF, and XML formats are used. The kinds of content delivered by a web feed are typically HTML or links to web pages and other digital media.

Web hosting service. A company that provides space on a server where individuals and business clients may store their websites. Web hosting services generally also sell other services, such as internet connectivity, domain names, tracking website data, file transfer protocols, and more.

Web syndication. Making a portion of a website available to other sites or individual subscribers. This could be simply by licensing the content so that other people can use it. However, in general, web syndication refers to making web feeds available from a site in order to provide other people with a summary of the site's recently added content (for example, the latest news or forum posts).

Although the format of web syndication could be anything transported over HTTP—such as HTML or JavaScript—it is more commonly XML. The two main families of web syndication formats are RSS and Atom.

Webcast. Sending audio and/or video live over the internet. A webcast uses streaming media technology to distribute nonstreaming media like radio and television over telecommunications networks. The ability to webcast using cheap and accessible technology has allowed independent media to flourish.

Web log. See *Blog*.

Whuffie. A reputation currency, or digital reputation. Users earn whuffie as people credit them for accomplishments.

Widget. An application that can be embedded into a website or blog, such as *blogroll* or scrolling headlines. Other people can take the widget customized on the site and put it on theirs; the originators get free advertising when others run their widgets.

Wikis. A collection of web pages editable by any reader. Wikis use extremely simple linking and formatting commands rather than requiring people to learn HTML. Wikis support hyperlinks and have a simple text syntax for creating new pages and cross-links between internal pages.

Like many simple concepts, "open editing" has some profound and subtle effects on Wiki usage. Allowing everyday users to create and edit any page in a website encourages democratic use of the web and promotes content composition by nontechnical users. Most wikis today still require technical knowledge to install and manage, but this is changing rapidly.

XML. A text markup language used for interchange of structured data; similar to HTML, except that it can be customized as needed for a variety of applications.

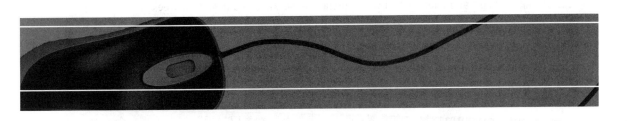

Index